Real Food for
People with Diabetes

REVISED

Also by Doris Cross

Fat Free & Ultra Lowfat Recipes

Almost Fat Free Down-Home Cooking

Doris' Fat-Free Homestyle Cooking

Real Italian Food for People with Diabetes

Real Mexican Food for People with Diabetes

Real Food for People with Diabetes

REVISED

Doris Cross

with Alice Williams

 THREE RIVERS PRESS • NEW YORK

Published by Three Rivers Press, New York, New York. Member of the Crown Publishing Group, a division of Random House, Inc. www.crownpublishing.com

THREE RIVERS PRESS and the Tugboat design are registered trademarks of Random House, Inc.

Originally published by Prima Publishing, Roseville, California, in 2001.

On the cover: Chuckwagon Cheeseburger (page 100), Oven French Fries (page 55), and Cherry Cobbler (page 230).

DISCLAIMER   A per serving nutritional breakdown is provided for each recipe. If a range is given for an ingredient amount, the breakdown is based on the smaller number. If a range is given for servings, the breakdown is based on the larger number. If a choice of ingredients is given in an ingredient listing, the breakdown is calculated using the first choice. Nutritional content may vary depending on the specific brands or types of ingredients used. "Optional" ingredients or those for which no specific amount is stated are not included in the breakdown. Nutritional figures are rounded to the nearest whole number.

Illustrations by Mary Rich

Printed in the United States of America

Library of Congress Cataloging-in-Publication Data
Cross, Doris.
    Real food for people with diabetes / Doris Cross, Alice Williams. — Rev.
      p.   cm.
    Includes index.
    1. Diabetes — Diet therapy — Recipes.   I. Williams, Alice.   II. Title.
RC662.C76   2000
616.4'620654 — dc21   00-049204
                                                                          CIP

ISBN 0-7615-2742-7

10 9 8 7 6 5 4

Second Edition

To Abby and Hannah

Contents

Soups, Salads, and Vegetables   35

Main Dishes and Casseroles   87

Pies, Pastries, and Desserts   207

Foreword

Perhaps you are one of the 16 million Americans with diabetes. Or maybe you have a family member with the disease. Perhaps you're simply watching your fat and sugar intake in an effort to reduce your risk of diabetes, heart disease, obesity, or cancer. Whatever your goals, you've opened a helpful recipe resource.

I have had the pleasure of knowing Doris Cross's work since 1991, when one of our cardiac rehabilitation patients at Saint John Medical Center in Tulsa, Oklahoma, brought in her first cookbook. At that time, true lowfat and fat-free products were becoming available, and many of our patients and staff were striving for daily fat intake as low as 10 percent of total calories. In an effort to provide our patients with ultra-lowfat recipes that tasted good and were easy to prepare, our Therapeutic Exercise Services staff at Saint John began to experiment and serve one another lowfat creations, often using recipes from Doris's first book. Word of these great-tasting healthful recipes quickly spread to our patients, and soon our monthly Taste 'n Tell Luncheons were born. These luncheons, which currently serve as many as 200, offer delicious meals containing 10 grams of fat or less, along with recipes to take home. Doris's recipes have been the highlight of many of these luncheons.

I have also used a number of Doris's recipes on our local CBS affiliate, KOTV, which broadcasts weekly lowfat recipes on both its *Six in the Morning* show and 5 o'clock evening news program. As I tell the viewers and my class participants at Saint John, my husband Jeff prefers high-fat food and is often skeptical of anything lowfat. If a lowfat creation passes the "Jeff test," anyone would probably love it! I can say without hesitation that Doris has conquered Jeff's taste buds time and time again.

And taste isn't Doris's only forte. My clients are always happy to find that you don't have to be a gourmet chef or shop at expensive specialty stores to use her books. She is a pro at creating practical, easy-to-use versions of our old, high-fat favorites.

Doris's recipes can be worked into almost any low-fat, low-sugar meal plan. Remember though, that portion sizes are still important and that dessert items should be used in moderation. Just because a recipe is healthy doesn't mean you can eat all you want. I like to refer to the U.S.D.A.'s food guide pyramid: Eat more plant foods — grains, fruits, and vegetables — and less animal foods, fats, and sweets.

I am looking forward to trying Doris's latest recipes and hope you will too. I have already had a sneak peak and tried the Hearty Ranch Biscuit Bake. It was fantastic! And yes, it passed the Jeff test.

—Janet L. Potts, R.D., L.D.

Acknowledgments

My most important thanks goes to Alice Williams, my co-author for this book. She is the most wonderful cook and worked hard to make sure these recipes were tasty. We had loads of fun testing dishes and eating our way through this project.

My next big thanks goes to my physician, Dr. Kathleen Harder, and her nurse, Jeannie Drew. It is so refreshing to find a doctor who cares as much as Dr. Harder. She and Jeannie were always so willing to take the time to work with me, seeing me through my ups and downs, and nail me to the wall when I needed it. With my busy schedule and just the smallest stubborn streak, I am probably not the easiest person to work with. I appreciate them both for their time and patience.

I am quite aware that this cookbook and all my others would not have been possible without the help of Hugh Merrill. He's a computer whiz who is good-hearted enough to help those who are "computer-challenged." I will always be grateful to him and his wife, Kathy, and their daughter, Rhonda, for all their help. Also, a special thanks to Stacy Croft for helping me with proofreading.

To Adran Wagner, my CPA, I can never thank you enough. Your expertise saved my sanity this year. You are the best!

A very special thanks goes to so many of my friends for their continued support during my cookbook ventures: Rick and Rodette Green, Staci Green, Michael Morgan, Janelle Walker, Amy Meyer, Kevin Miller, and Brandon Barnes. Thanks also to: Maurice Gershon, my son Bill and daughter-in-law Diana, my nephew and his wife, Tony and Traci Nelson, my cousins Gale and LaRue Davidson, Trena and Todd Hamilton, and Ron Wittwer.

Both of us would like to thank Alice's fellow teachers at Richmond Elementary for their tasting and critiques, and our friends Gina Morris and Lisa Coburn for the fun and laughter they bring to our lives.

Thank you to Janet Potts, R.D., for writing the foreword for this book and sharing her knowledge with me.

And of course, I love everyone at Prima Publishing in Roseville, California. They are all such fantastic people to work with, especially my editors Jamie Miller and Dawn Lairamore. I have always had such wonderful experiences working with the many great people at Prima and I appreciate all of them so much!

Notes

Note from Doris

Dear Friends:

In the fall of 1996 I went to my doctor with some health concerns and came home with a diagnosis of type II diabetes. I knew that I should not be surprised, considering my family's medical history. The surprising part was the latest research findings showing I was not alone: An estimated eight million Americans are now undiagnosed diabetics.

During the first days following my diagnosis I visited bookstores, looking for books that would help me understand what changes I would have to make. It was a challenge, and I felt eager to meet it with energy and a positive attitude. I progressed very well for the first month or two . . . then reality set in!

Suddenly the feeling of loss hit me. I had been a "sweets freak" for almost all of my life, and now I was being told that I couldn't have all the sugar I wanted? How could this be happening to me? I entered a phase of self-pity, thinking of all the years I had spent battling my weight. I had always depended on lowfat sweets to satisfy my cravings, but now what could I have?

During this time, I ran into an old friend whom I had not seen for over a year. As we visited, she remarked that she had been diagnosed with diabetes. Through my conversation with her, I began to understand that what I was feeling was very normal. It was then that I had a realization: If I had been able to create interesting and tasty recipes for my lowfat cookbooks, why not do the same with sugar-free foods? I was not the only person with diabetes searching for good recipes. So I began working immediately, determined to meet the challenge. It is my sincere hope that this book meets a real need in diabetics who are longing for the rich tastes of foods we are supposed to leave behind. I spent a lot of time especially on the desserts, since that is the food I most crave.

If you are not familiar with my previous three cookbooks, you might be interested, even though they are not written specfically for diabetics. They are available nationwide in major book stores:

Fat Free & Ultra Lowfat Recipes
Almost Fat Free Down-Home Cooking
Doris' Fat-Free Homestyle Cooking

I would also like to share information about some outstanding products I have come across during my years in the weight-loss business. These products are my absolute favorites, and I hope you will try them!

Cabot Farms 75% Reduced Fat Cheddar Cheese: This is a most heavenly white Cheddar cheese with only $2\frac{1}{2}$ grams of fat per ounce. This cheese tastes like full-fat Cheddar and grates and melts beautifully. For quality and taste, I have not found an equal on the market today. This product is widely available on the east coast; but if you live elsewhere, you may get it by mail order. I think it is worth the extra effort to order it! To contact Cabot Farms' mail-order department: (800) 639-3198.

Buttermist cooking spray is a butter-flavored nonstick spray that tastes wonderful! It is my all-time favorite spray. . . . I use it every day, and I'm not sure I could live without it! It has about the same number of calories and grams of fat as other cooking sprays, but the difference is in the taste. Spray it on toast, bagels, English muffins, popcorn . . . anything that needs "butter." This product is not water based, so it won't make your toast or popcorn soggy. The flavor is best if bread items are sprayed before toasting.

Buttermist cannot be found in supermarkets. Because it is so good, and not available in stores, I decided to make it available by shipping it through mail-order so other people could enjoy it, too. The cans are 14-ounce industrial size.

To order Buttermist by Visa or Mastercard, call (888) 743-0989 and leave your order on the answering machine. To order by mail, send a check for $15.50, which includes shipping and handling, for two 14-ounce cans to the following address. (Sorry, we are not allowed to ship to Canada.)

Steve's Books & Magazines
2612 S. Harvard Avenue
Tulsa, OK 74114

Remember when shopping . . . read labels, check grams of fat—especially saturated fat—and note the grams of carbohydrate and sugar and calorie count in each product.

As far as planning and eating meals, the best advice I can give you is to watch your quantities and serving sizes. Serving size is something I will always have to make a conscious effort to control. When I was growing up, serving dishes were on the table, so they could easily be passed around for second and third helpings. Now I find it easier to fill my plate before I sit down to eat; and no going back for seconds!

As most diabetics already know, the keys to health lie in lifestyle changes: Wise choices in cooking and eating; exercising; and don't forget to laugh! Look for the good things in life, and you'll find them all around you.

Best wishes,
Doris

Note from Alice

When Doris asked me to be involved in this book, I refused. Her first three cookbooks were all fantastic successes—why in the world would she need my help? She finally convinced me, and I am very grateful to her for so generously including me in this venture. (I am also impressed with her tolerance of my procrastination skills, which I have honed to a fine art.)

We are excited about this book of recipes we bring you. We know that it is not easy to be told to change the way you eat, and our goal has been to create delicious choices for your new eating life. Perhaps the most fun challenge has been to take old favorites from our artery-clogged pasts, and make them nutritionally acceptable *without* losing any of the "good stuff." We hope you enjoy making and eating what's in this book as much as we enjoyed thinking it up and putting it together!

I will always be appreciative of the healthful cooking and eating lessons my mother gave me; and I forgive her for all those times she served boiled celery. I especially enjoyed the years I spent cooking for my four sons as they grew up, even though it meant cooking those occasional frog legs. Jeff, Doug, Adam, and Ben—you guys are wonderful! Thanks for being mine!

Happy cooking!

Alice

Note About Equal

For easier measuring, use Equal Spoonful sweetener, instead of the Equal packets, for the recipes on the following pages: 2, 4, 6, 9, 11, 14, 17, 33, 46, 69, 124, 158, 209, 210, 212, 214, 216, 218, 220, 222, 224, 225, 226, 228, 232, 233, 234, 236, 238, 240, 242, 244, 246, 248, 250, 252, 254, 256, 258, 260, 262, 264, 266, 267, 268, 270, 272, 273, 274, 276, 278, 280, and 282.

Please do not use Equal for Recipes for the recipes listed above as the specified amounts are based on using Equal packets or Equal Spoonful.

Appetizers, Dips, Sauces, and Breads

Almond Bran Muffins

Apple Bran Muffins

Banana Muffins

Apricot Muffins

Doris's Banana Nut Muffins

Chili Cheese Dip

Cinnamon Crisps

Cinnamon Raisin Biscuits

Cream Cheese Roll with Orange Glaze

Corn Fritters

Date Nut Bran Muffins

Dilly Bread

Garlic and Poppy Seed Cheese Bread

Garlic Cheese Toast

Old-Fashioned Gravy

Pumpkin Bran Muffins

Jalapeño Cream Cheese Dip

Savory Chicken Dip

Cheese and Veggie Biscuit Loaf

Chocolate Chip Orange Muffins

Clam Dip

Fresh Cantaloupe with Orange Cream Sauce

Almond Bran Muffins

---◆---

These muffins have a delicious flavor—especially when eaten fresh from the oven.

Nonfat nonstick cooking spray
1 ½ cups reduced-fat Bisquick baking mix
1 cup Kellogg's Complete Bran Flakes cereal
2 ½ tablespoons powdered buttermilk
¼ cup fat-free liquid egg product
1 ½ teaspoons vanilla
½ cup evaporated skim milk
¼ cup water
⅓ cup sliced almonds
1 ¼ teaspoons almond extract
½ teaspoon Molly McButter dry butter flavor sprinkles*
¼ cup unsweetened applesauce
½ cup Equal sweetener
¼ teaspoon Sweet 'n Low sweetener

*This can be found in small bottles in the baking supplies section of the market.

Preheat oven to 375 degrees F

Spray twelve-muffin tin with cooking spray. In medium bowl, combine all ingredients and stir with spoon. Fill each muffin cup about one-fourth full. Bake at 375 degrees F for 20 minutes. Remove and serve; or cool and store in air-tight container to preserve freshness.

Recipe makes 12 muffins.

Each muffin provides:

135	Calories	2.5 g	Fat
11.6 g	Protein	0.37 g	Saturated fat
16.6 g	Carbohydrate	1 mg	Cholesterol

Diabetic exchanges: Starch, $1^{1}/_{2}$; fat, $^{1}/_{2}$

Apple Bran Muffins

—⚜—

Great to make ahead . . . and eat on the go! This is a lovely, moist muffin.

Nonfat nonstick cooking spray
1½ cups reduced-fat Bisquick baking mix
1 cup Kellogg's Complete Bran Flakes cereal
½ cup Equal sweetener
¼ teaspoon Sweet 'n Low sweetener
1 tablespoon powdered buttermilk
1 teaspoon vanilla
½ cup unsweetened applesauce
1½ teaspoons cinnamon
½ cup evaporated skim milk
¼ cup fat-free liquid egg product
½ teaspoon Molly McButter dry butter flavor sprinkles*

*This can be found in small bottles in the baking supplies section of the market.

Preheat oven to 375 degrees F

Spray muffin tin with cooking spray. Combine all ingredients in medium bowl and stir with spoon. Fill each muffin cup about one-fourth full. Bake at 375 degrees F for 20 minutes. Remove and serve; or cool and store in air-tight container to preserve freshness.

Recipe makes 12 muffins.

Each muffin provides:

120	Calories	1.2 g	Fat
10.9 g	Protein	0.23 g	Saturated fat
16.4 g	Carbohydrate	1 mg	Cholesterol

Diabetic exchanges: Starch, 1¹/₂; fat, ¹/₄

Banana Muffins

Seems like everyone loves banana muffins, which is why we just keep coming up with more recipes for them! Here is a yummy, sugar-free version that is quick and easy.

1 3/4 cups flour
1 1/2 teaspoons baking soda
1/4 teaspoon salt
1/2 teaspoon cream of tartar
2 tablespoons Equal sweetener
1/2 cup fat-free liquid egg product
1/2 cup plain nonfat yogurt
1/4 cup canola oil
1/4 cup applesauce
1/4 cup chopped nuts
1 to 2 ripe bananas, mashed
12 paper muffin-cup liners

Preheat oven to 400 degrees F

In large mixing bowl, mix flour, baking soda, salt, cream of tartar, and sweetener. In separate bowl, mix well the egg product, yogurt, oil, applesauce, nuts, and bananas. Pour over flour mixture and blend until moistened. Spoon batter into paper-lined muffin cups. Bake at 400 degrees F for 20 to 25 minutes.

Recipe makes 12 muffins.

Each muffin provides:

156	Calories	6.3 g	Fat
6.7 g	Protein	0.51 g	Saturated fat
18.3 g	Carbohydrate	0 mg	Cholesterol

Diabetic exchanges: Starch, 1¹/₂; fat, 1

Apricot Muffins

—✥—

Absolutely delicious!

Nonfat nonstick cooking spray
3 cups reduced-fat Bisquick baking mix
2 teaspoons Molly McButter dry butter flavor sprinkles*
1 teaspoon baking powder
12 packets Equal sweetener
3/4 cup fat-free liquid egg product
1 cup fat-free plain yogurt
1/4 cup orange juice
1/2 cup light apricot preserves

Preheat oven to 400 degrees F

Spray muffin tin with cooking spray. In large mixing bowl, combine baking mix, butter flavor sprinkles, baking powder, and sweetener. In small mixing bowl, beat together egg product, yogurt, orange juice, and apricot preserves until smooth. Make a well in center of dry ingredients and pour apricot mixture into it. Stir just until moist. Spoon into muffin tins, filling each one about two-thirds full. Bake at 400 degrees F for 15 minutes.

Recipe makes 12 muffins.

Each muffin provides:

155	Calories	2 g	Fat
5.6 g	Protein	0.40 g	Saturated fat
27.9 g	Carbohydrate	0 mg	Cholesterol

Diabetic exchanges: Starch, 1 3/4; fat, 2/5

· *This can be found in small bottles in the baking supplies section of the market.

Doris's Banana Nut Muffins

Fabulous flavor! The cereal in these muffins is Doris's favorite, so she figured it *had* to make great muffins.

Nonfat nonstick cooking spray
1 1/2 cups Post Banana Nut Crunch cereal
1 cup reduced-fat Bisquick baking mix
1/2 cup Equal sweetener
1/4 teaspoon Sweet 'n Low sweetener
1 tablespoon powdered buttermilk
1 1/2 teaspoons vanilla
1/2 teaspoon Molly McButter dry butter flavor sprinkles*
1/4 cup unsweetened applesauce
1/4 cup fat-free liquid egg product
3/4 cup skim milk

Preheat oven to 375 degrees F

Spray muffin tin with cooking spray. In medium bowl, combine all ingredients and stir with spoon. Let batter stand 10 minutes and stir again. Fill each muffin cup about one-fourth full. Bake at 375 degrees F for 20 minutes. Remove and serve warm; or cool and store in air-tight container to preserve freshness.

Recipe makes 12 muffins.

Each muffin provides:

117	Calories	1.6 g	Fat
10.5 g	Protein	0.29 g	Saturated fat
14.4 g	Carbohydrate	1 mg	Cholesterol

Diabetic exchanges: Starch, 1 3/4; fat, 1/5

---

*This can be found in small bottles in the baking supplies section of the market.

Chili Cheese Dip

What could be easier? . . . This dip is ready in less than five minutes. A real crowd pleaser for a party. Serve with baked chips or crackers.

1 can (15 ounces) turkey chili
3 fresh green onions, chopped
¹/₃ cup Tostitos restaurant-style cheese dip
   (*salsa con queso*)*

Pour turkey chili into a medium bowl and warm in microwave for 2 to 3 minutes. Remove and stir in chopped green onions. Add cheese and stir.

Recipe makes 6 servings.

Each serving provides:

85	Calories	2.1 g	Fat
6.4 g	Protein	0.84 g	Saturated fat
10.7 g	Carbohydrate	16 mg	Cholesterol

Diabetic exchanges: Starch, ³/₄; fat, ¹/₂

---

*This can be found in a jar in the chips section of the market.

Cinnamon Crisps

———❦———

A wonderfully yummy snack treat!

Nonfat nonstick cooking spray
3 (7-inch) fat-free flour tortillas
$^{1}/_{2}$ cup Equal sweetener
1$^{1}/_{2}$ teaspoons cinnamon
$^{1}/_{2}$ teaspoon Molly McButter dry butter flavor sprinkles*
2 egg whites, slightly beaten

Preheat oven to 375 degrees F

Spray large baking sheet with cooking spray. Using kitchen scissors, cut tortillas in half. (It is easy to cut several at one time.) Cut each half into pie-shaped thirds. In small bowl, combine Equal, cinnamon, and butter flavor sprinkles. Mix well with a spoon. Dip each tortilla piece first in egg white, then in cinnamon mixture, and place on baking sheet. Repeat procedure for all tortilla pieces. Bake at 375 degrees F for 14 to 15 minutes. Be sure not to *under*cook or they will be tough instead of crispy.

Recipe makes 18 chips. One serving equals 6 chips.

Each serving provides:

192	Calories	0.4 g	Fat
36.1 g	Protein	0.01 g	Saturated fat
13.4 g	Carbohydrate	0 mg	Cholesterol

Diabetic exchanges: Starch, 1$^{3}/_{4}$; lean protein, 1

---

*This can be found in small bottles in the baking supplies section of the market.

Cinnamon Raisin Biscuits

—⁂—

Delicious eaten hot from the oven.

Nonfat nonstick cooking spray
$1/3$ cup skim milk
$1/4$ cup raisins
2 cups reduced-fat Bisquick baking mix, additional for
    dusting work surface
$1^1/2$ teaspoons cinnamon
8 packets Equal sweetener
1 teaspoon Molly McButter dry butter flavor sprinkles*
$3/4$ cup plain nonfat yogurt
1 teaspoon vanilla

Preheat oven to 400 degrees F

Spray large baking sheet with cooking spray. Heat milk
and pour over raisins in medium bowl. Allow to sit 5 to 10
minutes. In large mixing bowl, stir together baking mix,
cinnamon, sweetener, and butter flavor sprinkles. Add

*This can be found in small bottles in the baking supplies section of the market.

yogurt and vanilla to raisin mixture. Stir into dry ingredients, mixing just until moist. Dust clean, dry surface with baking mix and turn dough out onto it (dough will be soft). Pat out to ¹/₂- to 1-inch thickness and cut with biscuit cutters. Place 1 inch apart on baking pan. Bake at 400 degrees F for 12 to 15 minutes. Serve hot.

Recipe makes 8 biscuits. One serving equals 1 biscuit.

Each serving provides:

149	Calories	2.0 g	Fat
4.9 g	Protein	0.42 g	Saturated fat
27.0 g	Carbohydrate	1 mg	Cholesterol

Diabetic exchanges: Starch, 1¹/₂; fat, ¹/₂

Cream Cheese Roll with Orange Glaze

This delectable roll will be ready in a jiffy! Wonderful for breakfast with coffee.

Filling
1 tub (8 ounces) fat-free cream cheese
1 egg white
$1/2$ teaspoon vanilla
$1/8$ teaspoon Molly McButter dry butter flavor sprinkles*
$1/8$ teaspoon lemon juice
1 teaspoon Sweet 'n Low sweetener

Crust for Roll
Nonfat nonstick cooking spray
1 can (8 ounces) refrigerated crescent rolls**
1 tablespoon sugar

Glaze
$1/4$ cup frozen orange juice concentrate, thawed
$1/4$ cup Equal sweetener
$1/8$ teaspoon vanilla

*This can be found in small bottles in the baking supplies section of the market.

**The cheapest brands usually have the lowest number of grams of fat. The ones we use have 3 grams of fat per serving.

Preheat oven to 350 degrees F

In medium bowl, blend cream cheese until smooth. Add egg white, vanilla, butter flavor sprinkles, lemon juice, and Sweet 'n Low. Mix well.

Spray large baking sheet with cooking spray. Remove dough from can and roll into ball with hands. Place dough on flat surface and roll out with rolling pin to about the size of a large dinner plate. Sprinkle with sugar. Spread filling over surface of dough and gently roll up loosely. Place roll on baking sheet and bake at 350 degrees F for 35 to 40 minutes.

While roll bakes, mix orange juice, Equal sweetener, and vanilla for glaze. When roll is done, allow to cool about 10 minutes. Drizzle glaze over top. Slice to serve.

Recipe makes 8 servings.

Each serving provides:

170	Calories	3.2 g	Fat
13.0 g	Protein	0.22 g	Saturated fat
20.6 g	Carbohydrate	3 mg	Cholesterol

Diabetic exchanges: Lean meat, 1; starch, 1 1/2

Corn Fritters

We both have fond memories of eating corn fritters way back when we were children. Of course, in the 1950s our mothers cheerfully fried recipes such as this in huge amounts of fat. This lean version of a favorite recipe retains all the nostalgic flavors we remember.

1 cup reduced-fat Bisquick biscuit mix
½ cup yellow cornmeal
¼ teaspoon salt
¼ cup fat-free liquid egg product
1 cup skim milk
½ cup canned or frozen corn
Nonfat nonstick cooking spray

Combine biscuit mix, cornmeal, salt, egg product, and milk in medium mixing bowl. Mix until smooth, then stir in corn. Spray large skillet with cooking spray and spoon batter into it as you would pancakes. Turn when bubbles appear. Serve warm with syrup.

Recipe makes about 12 fritters.

Each fritter provides:

147	Calories	1.8 g	Fat
5.1 g	Protein	0.33 g	Saturated fat
27.3 g	Carbohydrate	1 mg	Cholesterol

Diabetic exchanges: Starch, 1½; fat, ½

Date Nut Bran Muffins

———❧———

Yummy — a delicious breakfast muffin!

Nonfat nonstick cooking spray
1 cup Bran Buds or Kellogg's Complete Bran Flakes cereal
1 1/2 cups reduced-fat Bisquick
3 tablespoons powdered buttermilk
1/2 cup Equal sweetener
1/4 teaspoon Sweet 'n Low sweetener
1/4 cup fat-free liquid egg product
1 cup skim milk
1 teaspoon vanilla
1/4 cup applesauce
1/4 cup chopped dates
1/4 cup chopped pecans, optional

Preheat oven to 375 degrees F

Spray muffin tin with cooking spray. In medium bowl, combine all ingredients and stir with spoon. Let batter stand for 10 minutes. Stir again. Use enough batter to fill each muffin cup about one-third full. Bake at 375 degrees F for 20 minutes. Remove and serve; or cool and store in air-tight container to preserve freshness.

Recipe makes 12 muffins.

Each muffin provides:

132	Calories	1.3 g	Fat
11.5 g	Protein	0.30 g	Saturated fat
18.9 g	Carbohydrate	1 mg	Cholesterol

Diabetic exchanges: Lean protein, 1; starch, 1

Dilly Bread

We love the taste and texture of this bread, and it is wonderfully simple to make.

1 package (¼ ounce) dry yeast
¼ cup warm water
1 cup low fat (1 percent) cottage cheese
2 tablespoons sugar
2 tablespoons dill seed
1 tablespoon grated onion
¼ cup fat-free liquid egg product
1 teaspoon salt
¼ teaspoon baking soda
2¼ to 2½ cups flour
Nonfat nonstick cooking spray

Preheat oven to 350 degrees F

Dissolve yeast in the warm water. In large mixing bowl, combine cottage cheese, sugar, dill, onion, egg product, salt, and soda. Add yeast mixture to mixing bowl, stirring to combine. Gradually stir in flour to make a stiff dough.

Place dough in large bowl and cover tightly. Let rise until double in bulk. Shape into 2 small loaves and place on greased cookie sheet sprayed with cooking spray. Allow to rise again. Bake at 350 degrees F until lightly browned, about 30 minutes.

Recipe makes 2 small loaves with 6 slices per loaf. One serving equals 1 slice.

Each serving provides:

115	Calories	0.6 g	Fat
5.6 g	Protein	0.17 g	Saturated fat
21.6 g	Carbohydrate	1 mg	Cholesterol

Diabetic exchange: Starch, 1½

Garlic and Poppy Seed Cheese Bread

Anything so simple should not be this good! This is great with soup and/or salad.

Nonfat nonstick cooking spray
1 package (8 ounces) Boboli pizza crusts, 2 small crusts
    per package
Garlic powder
1 cup shredded Kraft fat-free mozzarella
1 teaspoon poppy seeds

Preheat oven to 425 degrees F

Spray large baking sheet and the tops of each crust with cooking spray. Sprinkle each crust with garlic powder and shredded cheese. Distribute the poppy seeds on top and place on baking sheet. Bake at 425 degrees F for 10 to 13 minutes or until cheese is melted.

Recipe makes 4 servings.

Each serving provides:

194	Calories	3.8 g	Fat
15.6 g	Protein	0.52 g	Saturated fat
25.7 g	Carbohydrate	8 mg	Cholesterol

Diabetic exchanges: Starch, 2; fat, 3/4

Garlic Cheese Toast

———⚸———

You will love this! Just the thing to go with soup and salad.

Nonfat nonstick cooking spray
$1/3$ cup shredded fat-free Cheddar cheese
1 tablespoon light sour cream
1 tablespoon fat-free mayonnaise
$1/4$ teaspoon minced garlic
4 medium to small slices sourdough bread

Preheat broiler

Spray baking sheet with cooking spray. In small bowl, mix cheese, sour cream, mayonnaise, and garlic. Stir until well blended. Place bread on baking sheet and toast on both sides under broiler. Remove and spread each with cheese spread. Return to broiler just long enough to melt the cheese. Be careful not to burn them!

Recipe makes 4 servings.

Each serving provides:

97	Calories	0.7 g	Fat
5.2 g	Protein	0.53 g	Saturated fat
17.2 g	Carbohydrate	3 mg	Cholesterol

Diabetic exchanges: Starch, 1; fat, $1/2$

Old-Fashioned Gravy

———&———

You won't believe how good this is! Try it with mashed potatoes.

2 tablespoons cornstarch
^{1}/3 cup water
1 can (14^1/2 ounces) fat-free chicken broth
^{1}/3 cup 2-percent milk
2 teaspoons Molly McButter dry butter flavor sprinkles*
1 teaspoon Butter Buds butter flavor granules*
Dash of onion powder
Dash of garlic powder
Black pepper

In small bowl, mix cornstarch in water and stir until smooth. Pour chicken broth into small saucepan and heat over medium-high heat. Add milk, butter flavor sprinkles and granules, onion and garlic powders, and pepper to taste. After mixture is well heated, stir in cornstarch and continue to stir until gravy thickens.

*This can be found in small bottles in the baking supplies section of the market.

Note: This is a somewhat thin gravy. If you prefer a thicker gravy, add a little more cornstarch. You can also simmer mushrooms into this basic gravy to enjoy a different flavor.

Recipe makes 6 servings.

Each serving provides:

26	Calories	0.3 g	Fat
1.2 g	Protein	0.18 g	Saturated fat
4.4 g	Carbohydrate	1 mg	Cholesterol

Diabetic exchanges: Starch, $^1/_5$; lowfat milk, $^1/_{10}$

Pumpkin Bran Muffins

———— ✦ ————

These are *so* good, you won't notice how good for you they are.

Nonfat nonstick cooking spray
1 1/2 cups Kellogg's Complete Bran Flakes cereal
1 cup orange juice
1 1/2 cups all-purpose flour
2 teaspoons baking powder
1 teaspoon baking soda
1 teaspoon cinnamon
1/2 teaspoon salt
2 tablespoons canola oil
1/4 cup fat-free liquid egg product
1/2 cup canned pumpkin
1/4 cup plain nonfat yogurt
1/4 cup raisins

Preheat oven to 400 degrees F

Spray muffin tin with cooking spray. In small bowl, mix cereal in orange juice to soften. In medium bowl, combine flour, baking powder, baking soda, cinnamon, and salt. In large mixing bowl, combine oil, egg product, pumpkin, yogurt, and raisins. Stir in softened cereal. Add flour mixture, stirring just until moistened. Spoon mixture into tins, filling cups about two-thirds full. Bake at 400 degrees F for 20 minutes.

Recipe makes 12 large muffins.

Each muffin provides:

125	Calories	2.7 g	Fat
3.2 g	Protein	0.22 g	Saturated fat
22.6 g	Carbohydrate	0 mg	Cholesterol

Diabetic exchanges: Starch, $1^1/_4$; fat, $^1/_2$

Jalapeño Cream Cheese Dip

———— ✦ ————

A tasty dip with a bite! Serve with lowfat crackers
or chips.

1 tub (8 ounces) fat-free cream cheese
2 tablespoons jalapeño jelly
¼ cup finely chopped green pepper
1 teaspoon dry onion flakes or 3 green onions, chopped

Combine all ingredients in small bowl and stir until thoroughly mixed. Chill and serve.

Recipe makes 8 servings.

Each serving provides:

39	Calories	0.0 g	Fat
4.1 g	Protein	0.00 g	Saturated fat
4.7 g	Carbohydrate	5 mg	Cholesterol

Diabetic exchanges: Vegetable, 1; lean meat, ¼

Savory Chicken Dip

———— ✦ ————

This is a fantastic party dip but is also nice as an addition to a fruit plate or as a sandwich filling.

1 tub (8 ounces) fat-free cream cheese
1 tub (8 ounces) light cream cheese
1 cup chopped chicken breast meat
$^1/_4$ cup fat-free chicken broth
$^1/_4$ cup chopped onion
$^1/_4$ cup toasted chopped almonds, optional
$^1/_4$ teaspoon ground savory
$^1/_4$ teaspoon ground thyme
$^1/_4$ teaspoon white pepper
$^1/_2$ teaspoon lemon juice

Blend all ingredients together in food processor until smooth. Chill several hours or overnight.

Recipe makes about 8 servings. One serving equals $^1/_4$ cup.

Each serving provides:

118	Calories	5.7 g	Fat
12.5 g	Protein	3.21 g	Saturated fat
3.7 g	Carbohydrate	34 mg	Cholesterol

Diabetic exchanges: Lean meat, 2

Cheese and Veggie Biscuit Loaf

——⚬🎔⚬——

This is so pretty, and delicious, too! It is a tasty bread to serve with soup or salad.

1 cup shredded fresh carrots
1 cup frozen chopped broccoli
$1/2$ cup frozen chopped spinach
1 small fresh zucchini, chopped
1 small yellow squash, chopped
1 cup fat-free grated Cheddar or American cheese
$2^1/2$ cups reduced-fat Bisquick baking mix
$1/2$ cup skim milk
1 teaspoon Molly McButter dry butter flavor sprinkles*
1 tablespoon dry onion flakes
$1/3$ cup fat-free liquid egg product
Nonfat nonstick cooking spray

*This can be found in small bottles in the baking supplies section of the market.

Preheat oven to 375 degrees F

In large bowl, mix carrots, broccoli, spinach, zucchini, and squash. Add cheese. In medium bowl, combine baking mix, skim milk, butter flavor sprinkles, onion flakes, and egg product and mix thoroughly. Add this mixture to the vegetables and stir by hand until well blended.

Spray bundt pan with cooking spray. Pour dough evenly into pan. Bake at 375 degrees F for 35 minutes. Remove and serve warm.

Recipe makes 10 servings.

Each serving provides:

158	Calories	2.1 g	Fat
8.3 g	Protein	0.65 g	Saturated fat
26.5 g	Carbohydrate	2 mg	Cholesterol

Diabetic exchanges: Starch, 1¹/₂; vegetable, 1; fat, ¹/₂

Chocolate Chip Orange Muffins

I can't begin to describe how wonderful these taste.

1½ cups all-purpose flour
¼ cup sugar
⅛ teaspoon salt
¼ cup milk chocolate chips
½ cup evaporated skim milk
¼ cup frozen orange juice concentrate, thawed
1 teaspoon orange peel, finely grated
2 egg whites, beaten
1 tablespoon canola oil
1 teaspoon vanilla
Nonfat nonstick cooking spray

Preheat oven to 400 degrees F

In large bowl, combine all dry ingredients and mix. Stir in chocolate chips. In another bowl, combine milk, orange juice concentrate, orange peel, egg whites, canola oil, and vanilla. Add liquid mixture to dry ingredients and stir until blended.

Spray 12-cup muffin pan with nonstick cooking spray and fill each cup about two-thirds full. Bake at 400 degrees F for 12 to 15 minutes.

Recipe makes 12 muffins.

Each muffin provides:

122	Calories	2.3 g	Fat
3.3 g	Protein	0.66 g	Saturated fat
22.1 g	Carbohydrate	1 mg	Cholesterol

Diabetic exchanges: Starch, 1; fruit, $^1/_2$; fat, $^1/_4$

Clam Dip

A big hit at parties.

1 can (6 ounces) minced clams, drained
1½ cups Kraft fat-free cream cheese
⅓ cup fat-free sour cream
4 to 5 drops Tabasco sauce
1 tablespoon dry onion flakes
1 clove garlic, pressed
½ teaspoon seasoned salt (optional)
2 tablespoons finely chopped canned mushrooms

Combine all ingredients in medium bowl and stir until thoroughly mixed. Chill and serve with lowfat crackers or chips.

Recipe makes 6 servings.

Each serving provides:

84	Calories	0.3 g	Fat
12.5 g	Protein	0.03 g	Saturated fat
7.0 g	Carbohydrate	18 mg	Cholesterol

Diabetic exchanges: Lean meat, ¾; skim milk, ½

Fresh Cantaloupe with Orange Cream Sauce

Refreshing and delightful.

³/₄ cup fat-free sour cream
2 tablespoons frozen orange juice concentrate
¹/₂ teaspoon fresh grated orange peel
¹/₂ teaspoon vanilla
2 tablespoons cold water
¹/₂ cup Equal sweetener
3¹/₂ cups of fresh peeled and chunked cantaloupe

In medium bowl, combine sour cream, frozen orange juice concentrate, grated orange peel, vanilla, water, and Equal. Use an electric mixer and mix on high until well blended. Pour sauce over cantaloupe chunks and serve.

Recipe makes 4 servings.

Each serving provides:

106	Calories	0.4 g	Fat
5.5 g	Protein	0.02 g	Saturated fat
22.1 g	Carbohydrate	0 mg	Cholesterol

Diabetic exchanges: Fruit, 1; skim milk, ¹/₂

Soups, Salads, and Vegetables

Broccoli Salad

Cheesy Broccoli and Rice

Carrot Raisin Salad

Very Cherry Salad

Cheesy Ham and Potato Chowder

Corn Pudding

Cranberry Chicken Salad

Creamy Fruit Salad

Creamy Potato Casserole

Velvety Carrot Soup

Crunchy Baked Eggplant

Aunt Ruth's Cucumber Dressing

Curry Macaroni Salad

Dilly Potato Salad

Oven French Fries

Green Beans and New Potatoes

Hominy Green Chili Cheese Bake

Harvard Beets

Fresh Asparagus in Lemon "Butter"

Old-Fashioned Mashed Potatoes

Picnic Macaroni Salad

Oklahoma Okra

Orange Carrots

Oriental Cucumbers

Green Beans with Roasted Onions

Crunchy Pea Salad

Sweet and Sour Rice Salad

Salsa Salad

Santa Fe Soup

Spicy Peanut Chicken Salad

Sauerkraut Salad

Summer Cucumber Salad

Veggie Pockets

Oriental Peanut Salad

Santa Fe Salad

Sweet and Sour Cabbage

Pasta Veggie Sauce

Southern Potato Salad

Restaurant-Style Potato Skins

Orange Crispy Sweet Potatoes

Fresh Vegetable Medley

Broccoli Salad

If you are feeding broccoli-haters, you just might win them over with this recipe. It has a nice blend of flavors and crunch . . . and it's good for you! May be chilled before serving, if desired.

1 large bunch broccoli, chopped
1 medium red onion, chopped
1/2 cup raisins
1 cup fat-free mayonnaise
12 packets Equal sweetener
2 tablespoons vinegar

In large mixing bowl, combine broccoli, onion, and raisins. In separate bowl, mix mayonnaise, sweetener, and vinegar, and pour over broccoli. Stir well and serve.

Recipe makes 8 to 10 servings.

Each serving provides:

63	Calories	0.2 g	Fat
2.8 g	Protein	0.04 g	Saturated fat
14.1 g	Carbohydrate	0 mg	Cholesterol

Diabetic exchange: Vegetable, 2 1/2

Cheesy Broccoli and Rice

This is the healthy version of a family favorite . . . and no one can tell the difference! Think about this dish the next time you need something for a potluck supper. It's what we call a "crowd pleaser."

Nonfat nonstick cooking spray
1 cup chopped celery
1 cup chopped onion
1 package (10 ounces) frozen chopped broccoli, thawed
1 can (10^3/$_4$ ounces) lowfat cream of chicken soup
2 tablespoons Molly McButter dry butter flavor sprinkles*
1 cup water
^{1}/$_2$ cup canned evaporated skim milk
1 cup Minute rice
1 cup shredded light Cheddar cheese
Pepper

*This can be found in small bottles in the baking supplies section of the market.

Preheat oven to 350 degrees F

Spray large skillet with cooking spray. Sauté celery and onion over medium-low heat for 10 minutes. Stir in broccoli and mix well. Cook 10 minutes more. Add chicken soup, butter sprinkles, water, milk, rice, cheese, and pepper, stirring well to combine thoroughly. Spray 2-quart casserole dish with cooking spray to prevent sticking and pour mixture into it. Cover and bake at 350 degrees F for 20 to 30 minutes.

Recipe makes 6 servings.

Each serving provides:

198	Calories	4.6 g	Fat
11 g	Protein	2.27 g	Saturated fat
27.9 g	Carbohydrate	19 mg	Cholesterol

Diabetic exchanges: Starch, 1; vegetable, 1; medium fat protein, 1

Carrot Raisin Salad

This old gem is straight from our childhoods. If you have fat grams to spare, a handful of peanuts is a mighty tasty addition.

2 cups grated carrots
1/3 cup raisins
1/3 cup fat-free mayonnaise or salad dressing
1 tablespoon orange juice

Combine ingredients in large salad bowl and serve!

Recipe makes 4 to 6 servings.

Each serving provides:

54	Calories	0.1 g	Fat
0.7 g	Protein	0.02 g	Saturated fat
13.6 g	Carbohydrate	0 mg	Cholesterol

Diabetic exchanges: Vegetable, 1; fruit, 1/2

Very Cherry Salad

—❧—

This salad absolutely bursts with flavor. The recipe makes a large amount, so think about it when you need a side dish for big holiday dinners. (Cousin Alice would like to thank Cousin Cindy for allowing her to steal this recipe and include it in this book.)

1 can (16 ounces) pitted tart cherries in water, retain juice
1 can (20 ounces) crushed pineapple, retain juice
3 cups juice (from canned cherries and pineapple, plus orange juice)
1 box (0.3 ounces) sugar-free cherry Jell-O
1 envelope Knox gelatin, dissolved in 1/4 cup water
9 packets Equal sweetener

Drain and measure juice from cans of cherries and pineapple and add enough orange juice to total 3 cups combined. In medium saucepan, heat juice until hot but not boiling. Pour into 4-quart serving dish (large mold, bowl, casserole, or other) and stir in Jell-O, gelatin, and sweetener until dissolved. Add fruits and stir. Chill 2 hours or until firm.

Recipe makes 12 servings.

Each serving provides:

76	Calories	0.1 g	Fat
2.7 g	Protein	0.03 g	Saturated fat
16.5 g	Carbohydrate	0 mg	Cholesterol

Diabetic exchanges: Fruit, 1; lean meat, 1/4

Cheesy Ham and Potato Chowder

If you are in the mood for comfort food that will warm the cockles of your heart, this is a great choice. Its creamy texture and rich flavor make it a year-round favorite at our houses.

3 medium potatoes, peeled and cubed
2 tablespoons flour
2 tablespoons Molly McButter dry butter flavor sprinkles*
1 tablespoon dry onion flakes
1/8 to 1/4 teaspoon pepper
2 cups fat-free milk
1/4 cup fat-free plain yogurt
6 slices fat-free American cheese
1/2 cup diced ham

*This can be found in small bottles in the baking supplies section of the market.

Cook potatoes in boiling water approximately 20 minutes or until tender. Drain and mash slightly and set aside. In large skillet or 4-quart saucepan, combine flour, butter flavor sprinkles, onion flakes, and pepper. Using a whisk, blend in milk and yogurt. Stirring constantly, cook over medium heat until thickened. Stir in cheese until melted. Add potatoes and ham to mixture and stir. Serve hot.

Recipe makes 4 servings.

Each serving provides:

234	Calories	1.2 g	Fat
17.7 g	Protein	0.45 g	Saturated fat
37.3 g	Carbohydrate	10 mg	Cholesterol

Diabetic exchanges: Skim milk, 1; starch, 1; lean meat, 1

Corn Pudding

—❧—

This is a nice, custardy, old-fashioned dish.

Nonfat nonstick butter-flavored cooking spray
1 tablespoon Molly McButter dry butter flavor sprinkles*
2 packets Equal sweetener
2 tablespoons flour
1 ³/₄ cups milk
1 carton (8 ounces) fat-free liquid egg product
2 cups cooked corn

Preheat oven to 325 degrees F

Spray 2-quart baking dish with cooking spray. In large mixing bowl, combine butter sprinkles, sweetener, and flour. Stir in milk, egg product, and corn. Mix until smooth. Pour mixture into baking dish. Bake at 325 degrees F for 45 minutes, stirring once 15 minutes into cooking time. Serve warm.

Recipe makes 4 to 6 servings.

Each serving provides:

111	Calories	1.7 g	Fat
7.8 g	Protein	0.89 g	Saturated fat
17.1 g	Carbohydrate	5 mg	Cholesterol

Diabetic exchanges: Starch, ¹/₂; low-fat milk, ¹/₂; vegetable, ¹/₂

---

*This can be found in small bottles in the baking supplies section of the market.

Cranberry Chicken Salad

—ⅆ—

A great luncheon salad. To serve, cut into squares and place on lettuce leaves. You might also add a dab of fat-free mayonnaise on top of each serving.

1 box (0.3 ounces) sugar-free cranberry Jell-O
1 cooked chicken breast (3 ounces), finely chopped
$^1/_2$ cup chopped celery
$^1/_2$ cup fat-free mayonnaise
$^1/_2$ teaspoon vinegar
Salt, optional

Prepare cranberry Jell-O according to directions on box. Set in refrigerator until syrupy (about 30 minutes). Add chopped chicken, celery, mayonnaise, vinegar, and optional salt, mixing well. Pour into $8^1/_2 \times 4^1/_2 \times 2^1/_2$-inch loaf pan or Jell-O mold and return to refrigerator. Chill until set, 2 to 3 hours.

Recipe makes 4 servings.

Each serving provides:

70	Calories	0.8 g	Fat
8.2 g	Protein	0.22 g	Saturated fat
6.7 g	Carbohydrate	18 mg	Cholesterol

Diabetic exchanges: Starch, $^1/_4$; lean meat, 1

Creamy Fruit Salad

Cool and delicious!

Fruit Salad
1 can (15 ounces) sliced light peaches, drained
1 can (8 ounces) pineapple tidbits, drained
1 can (15¼ ounces) tropical fruit, retain juice
1 package (16 ounces) frozen whole strawberries
    (no sugar added), partially thawed
2 cups frozen blueberries (no sugar added),
    partially thawed
1 can (8½ ounces) sliced pears, drained

Cream Sauce
1 tub (12 ounces) fat-free cream cheese
½ cup Equal sweetener
1½ teaspoons vanilla
Juice from can of tropical fruit

Place peaches, pineapple, tropical fruit, strawberries, blueberries, and pears in large bowl. Stir gently to mix. Set aside.

In medium bowl, combine cream cheese, Equal, and vanilla. Beat with electric mixer until thoroughly blended. Add juice from tropical fruit and beat until smooth. Pour this sauce over fruit and mix with spoon. Chill and serve.

Recipe makes 12 servings. One serving equals approximately ³/₄ cup.

Each serving provides:

125	Calories	0.3 g	Fat
12.7 g	Protein	0.02 g	Saturated fat
17.6 g	Carbohydrate	5 mg	Cholesterol

Diabetic exchange: Fruit, 2

Creamy Potato Casserole

———— ❧ ————

This is a perfect brunch dish.

1 pound frozen hash browns, thawed
1 can (10³/₄ ounces) cream of chicken soup
1 cup fat-free sour cream
¹/₂ cup chopped onion
1 cup grated fat-free Cheddar cheese
2 tablespoons Molly McButter dry butter flavor sprinkles*
¹/₈ teaspoon pepper
1 cup crushed cornflake crumbs

Preheat oven to 350 degrees F

Oil a 2-quart casserole dish. In large bowl, combine hash browns, soup, sour cream, onion, cheese, butter flavor sprinkles, and pepper. Pour into casserole dish and top with cornflake crumbs. Bake at 350 degrees F for 35 to 45 minutes.

Recipe makes 8 servings.

Each serving provides:

184	Calories	2.3 g	Fat
10 g	Protein	0.96 g	Saturated fat
30.1 g	Carbohydrate	6 mg	Cholesterol

Diabetic exchanges: Starch, 1 ¹/₂; lean protein, 1

---

*This can be found in small bottles in the baking supplies section of the market.

Velvety Carrot Soup

———— ❧ ————

This creamy, smooth soup has the most wonderful flavor.
Perfect with a salad for lunch. Sprinkle chopped peanuts
over top of soup to serve.

Nonfat nonstick butter-flavored cooking spray
1 medium onion, chopped
1 teaspoon minced garlic
3 cups fat-free chicken broth
1 teaspoon curry powder
1 tablespoon flour
4 large carrots, chopped
1 cup fat-free plain yogurt
1 tablespoon peanut butter

Spray large skillet with cooking spray. Over medium heat,
sauté onion 3 to 4 minutes. Add garlic and a few tablespoons of the chicken broth and sauté 2 to 3 minutes more.
Sprinkle curry powder and flour into skillet and blend well.
Add remaining chicken broth and carrots. Cover skillet and
simmer 15 minutes or until carrots are tender. Cool slightly
and pour mixture into food processor. Add yogurt and
peanut butter. Process until smooth. Serve warm or chilled.

Recipe makes 4 servings.

Each serving provides:

126	Calories	2.6 g	Fat
7.4 g	Protein	0.5 g	Saturated fat
19.4 g	Carbohydrate	1 mg	Cholesterol

Diabetic exchanges: Lean protein, 1; vegetable, 2

Crunchy Baked Eggplant

———— ❧ ————

For a long time we thought the only way anyone ever cooked eggplant was to dip it in egg, then crumbs, and fry it. Although we are now much more savvy about the ways of eggplant preparation, we still enjoy an occasional meal of crunchy eggplant slices.

Nonfat nonstick cooking spray
1 medium eggplant
1 cup fat-free mayonnaise
1 tablespoon lemon juice
1/4 teaspoon salt
1/4 teaspoon garlic powder
2 tablespoons skim milk
2 cups cornflake crumbs
1/4 cup grated fat-free Parmesan cheese

Preheat oven to 350 degrees F

Spray a large baking sheet with cooking spray. Peel eggplant, if desired, and slice into $\frac{1}{2}$-inch slabs. In a shallow bowl, combine mayonnaise, lemon juice, salt, garlic powder, and skim milk. In another shallow dish, stir together cornflake crumbs and Parmesan. Dip eggplant slices into mayonnaise mixture, then in cornflake crumb mixture to coat completely. Place slices on baking sheet and bake at 350 degrees F for 25 minutes.

Recipe makes 4 servings.

Each serving provides:

306	Calories	0.4 g	Fat
6.5 g	Protein	0.04 g	Saturated fat
71.1 g	Carbohydrate	3 mg	Cholesterol

Diabetic exchanges: Starch, 3; vegetable, 2

Aunt Ruth's
Cucumber Dressing

Alice's wonderful Aunt Ruth, who is perhaps the finest cook of all time, must receive credit for this zingy salad dressing.

$^1/_2$ cup pared, shredded cucumber
1 teaspoon grated onion
1 teaspoon vinegar
$^1/_2$ teaspoon sugar
$^1/_4$ teaspoon salt
$^1/_4$ teaspoon seasoned salt
Black pepper
1 cup plain nonfat yogurt

Drain and blot excess moisture from the shredded cucumber. Combine onion, vinegar, sugar, salt, seasoned salt, and black pepper to taste, and mix well. Gently fold in yogurt. Chill for several hours to allow flavors to blend. To serve, spoon dressing over salad.

Recipe makes 6 servings. One serving equals $^1/_4$ cup.

Each serving provides:

25	Calories	0.1 g	Fat
2.3 g	Protein	0.05 g	Saturated fat
3.7 g	Carbohydrate	1 mg	Cholesterol

Diabetic exchange: Vegetable, 1

Curry Macaroni Salad

———— ✧ ————

If you are looking for something different for your next picnic, try this yummy salad.

2 1/2 cups cooked macaroni
1/2 cup chopped celery
1 cup sliced red or green seedless grapes
4 green onions, chopped
1/3 cup fat-free mayonnaise
1 teaspoon Dijon mustard
1 teaspoon curry powder
1/2 teaspoon lemon juice
Salt

In large mixing bowl, stir together macaroni, celery, grapes, and onions. In small bowl, stir together mayonnaise, mustard, curry powder, and lemon juice. Add mayonnaise mixture to macaroni and stir gently to blend. Add salt if desired. Serve chilled or at room temperature.

Recipe makes 4 servings.

Each serving provides:

177	Calories	1.1 g	Fat
4.8 g	Protein	0.17 g	Saturated fat
37.5 g	Carbohydrate	0 mg	Cholesterol

Diabetic exchanges: Starch, 1 1/2; vegetable, 1; fruit, 1/2

Dilly Potato Salad

—❧—

This is a lovely, light potato salad with an absolutely delicious flavor.

$^1/_2$ cup 2-percent cottage cheese
$^1/_2$ cup plain nonfat yogurt
1 clove garlic, minced
1 teaspoon salt
$^1/_8$ teaspoon pepper
$^1/_2$ to 1 teaspoon dried dill weed
$^1/_2$ cup sliced green onions
1 cup diced cucumber
4 cups (3 large or 4 medium) cubed cooked potatoes

Combine all ingredients in large salad bowl and chill. Serve cold.

Recipe makes 6 servings.

Each serving provides:

111	Calories	0.5 g	Fat
5.5 g	Protein	0.29 g	Saturated fat
21.5 g	Carbohydrate	2 mg	Cholesterol

Diabetic exchanges: Starch, 1; vegetable, 1; skim milk, $^1/_{10}$

Oven French Fries

———— ❧ ————

Our favorite! These are so good, and you don't even have to feel guilty about eating them. Serve with lowfat hotdogs or hamburgers. Enjoy!

Nonfat nonstick butter-flavored cooking spray*
2 medium baking potatoes
Seasoned salt
Black pepper

Preheat oven to 375 degrees F

Spray large baking sheet with cooking spray. Peel potatoes, then slice into French-fry-sized pieces. Arrange potato pieces on baking sheet, close together but not touching. Spray potatoes with butter-flavored cooking spray. Sprinkle with seasoned salt and black pepper to taste. Bake at 375 degrees F for about 40 minutes or until browned.

Recipe makes 4 servings.

Each serving provides:

56	Calories	0.3 g	Fat
1.4 g	Protein	0.02 g	Saturated fat
12.3 g	Carbohydrate	0 mg	Cholesterol

Diabetic exchange: Starch, ⁴/₅

---

*We love Buttermist for this recipe.

Green Beans and New Potatoes

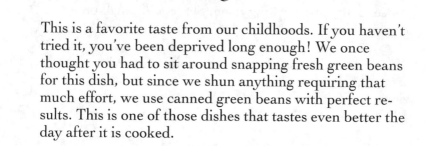

This is a favorite taste from our childhoods. If you haven't tried it, you've been deprived long enough! We once thought you had to sit around snapping fresh green beans for this dish, but since we shun anything requiring that much effort, we use canned green beans with perfect results. This is one of those dishes that tastes even better the day after it is cooked.

2 cans (15 ounces each) green beans
1 medium onion, chopped
3 slices turkey bacon, diced
Salt and black pepper
6 to 8 small new potatoes, scrubbed

Empty both cans of green beans into large saucepan. Add onion and turkey bacon. Season with salt and pepper. Cover pan and place over medium heat. Cook 30 to 45 minutes. Add new potatoes and reduce heat to low. Continue cooking another 30 to 45 minutes, until potatoes are tender.

Recipe makes 8 servings.

Each serving provides:

80	Calories	1.1 g	Fat
2.8 g	Protein	0.22 g	Saturated fat
15.7 g	Carbohydrate	4 mg	Cholesterol

Diabetic exchanges: Starch, 1/2; vegetable, 1; fat, 1/3

Hominy Green Chili Cheese Bake

Even folks who claim they don't like hominy will love this.

Nonfat nonstick cooking spray
1 can (16 ounces) hominy, drained
1 cup grated fat-free American or Cheddar cheese
1 cup fat-free sour cream
3 tablespoons canned, chopped green chilies
$^1/_4$ teaspoon salt

Preheat oven to 350 degrees F

Spray small (1-quart) casserole dish with cooking spray.
In medium bowl, combine all ingredients, then pour into
casserole dish. Bake at 350 degrees F for 20 to 30 minutes.

Recipe makes 4 servings.

Each serving provides:

112	Calories	0.1 g	Fat
13.9 g	Protein	0.6 g	Saturated fat
14 g	Carbohydrate	5 mg	Cholesterol

Diabetic exchanges: Starch, 1; lean protein, $^1/_2$

Harvard Beets

We think this is just about the *only* way to fix beets.

1 can (16 ounces) diced beets
1/2 cup beet liquid
1/2 cup vinegar
4 teaspoons cornstarch
Sugar substitute equivalent to 2 tablespoons sugar
Pinch of salt

Drain—but reserve 1/2 cup liquid from—can of beets. In medium saucepan, combine reserved liquid, vinegar, cornstarch, sugar substitute, and salt. Cook, stirring often over medium heat until thickened. Add beets and serve warm.

Recipe makes 4 servings.

Each serving provides:

56	Calories	0.1 g	Fat
0.9 g	Protein	0.01 g	Saturated fat
14.3 g	Carbohydrate	0 mg	Cholesterol

Diabetic exchanges: Starch, 1/3; vegetable, 1

Fresh Asparagus in Lemon "Butter"

Fresh asparagus is our favorite springtime treat. (Alice was tempted to say this recipe serves one person.)

¹/₂ ounce Butter Buds butter flavor granules*
¹/₂ cup hot water
1 tablespoon Molly McButter dry butter flavor sprinkles*
2 teaspoons fresh (or frozen, thawed) lemon juice
1 pound fresh asparagus

In small mixing bowl, whisk together butter granules, hot water, butter sprinkles, and lemon juice until blended. Steam asparagus and serve with butter sauce poured over the top.

Recipe makes 4 servings.

Each serving provides:

44	Calories	0.5 g	Fat
3 g	Protein	0.16 g	Saturated fat
8.4 g	Carbohydrate	0 mg	Cholesterol

Diabetic exchange: Vegetable, 2

---

*This can be found in small bottles in the baking supplies section of the market.

Old-Fashioned Mashed Potatoes

Mashed potatoes simply *have* to be our favorite food.
Serve these to crabby people, and they will smile again!

3 medium baking potatoes, peeled and cut into chunks
$^1/_2$ tablespoon Butter Buds butter flavor granules*
2 tablespoons Molly McButter dry butter flavor sprinkles*
$^1/_4$ cup 2-percent milk
Black pepper
Salt, optional

Place potato chunks in medium saucepan and add water
to tops of potatoes. Cover and cook over medium heat
until potatoes are tender, 20 to 25 minutes. Drain, then
add butter flavor granules, butter flavor sprinkles, milk,
and pepper. Beat with electric mixer until smooth. Taste
and add salt, if desired.

*This can be found in small bottles in the baking supplies section of the market.

Note: The amount of milk used depends on personal taste. You may want to add a little more or use a little less. And do not add salt until you taste; we don't think you will need any. Great served with meatloaf.

Recipe makes 6 servings.

Each serving provides:

73	Calories	0.3 g	Fat
1.5 g	Protein	0.15 g	Saturated fat
15.6 g	Carbohydrate	1 mg	Cholesterol

Diabetic exchange: Starch, 1

Picnic Macaroni Salad

——— ❧ ———

This salad just screams, "Take me on a picnic!"

2 ½ cups cooked macaroni
½ cup chopped dill pickle
½ cup chopped red or green bell pepper
½ cup chopped celery
3 green onions, chopped
⅓ cup fat-free mayonnaise
1 tablespoon dill pickle juice
1 packet Equal sweetener
½ teaspoon mustard
Salt

In large mixing bowl, stir together macaroni, pickle, pepper, celery, and onion. In small bowl, stir together mayonnaise, pickle juice, sweetener, and mustard, then add to macaroni mixture. Add salt to taste. Chill or serve at room temperature.

Recipe makes 4 servings.

Each serving provides:

155	Calories	0.7 g	Fat
4.7 g	Protein	0.11 g	Saturated fat
32.3 g	Carbohydrate	0 mg	Cholesterol

Diabetic exchanges: Starch, 1 ⅓; vegetable, 2

Oklahoma Okra

—❧—

When we meet folks from the north who don't know what okra is, we feel very sorry for them.

Nonfat nonstick butter-flavored cooking spray
1/2 cup chopped onion
1 green pepper, chopped
1 to 2 tablespoons Molly McButter dry butter flavor
    sprinkles*
1 1/2 cups canned diced tomatoes
1 1/2 cups sliced okra (fresh or frozen)
Salt and pepper

Spray large skillet with cooking spray. Sauté onion and green pepper over medium heat 4 to 5 minutes. Sprinkle butter flavor sprinkles over onion and green pepper and stir until dissolved. Add tomatoes and okra. Cover skillet and cook until okra is tender, 10 to 15 minutes. Add salt and pepper to taste.

Recipe makes 6 servings.

Each serving provides:

39	Calories	0.3 g	Fat
1.5 g	Protein	0.04 g	Saturated fat
8.3 g	Carbohydrate	0 mg	Cholesterol

Diabetic exchange: Vegetable, 1 1/2

---

*This can be found in small bottles in the baking supplies section of the market.

Orange Carrots

We think this recipe would make Dennis the Menace change his mind about carrots.

1 pound carrots, scrubbed
2 teaspoons cornstarch
2 packets Equal sweetener
1 cup orange juice
Salt and pepper, optional

Slice carrots and steam until just tender. In large saucepan, combine cornstarch, sweetener, orange juice, and optional salt and pepper. Stir well and cook over medium heat. Add carrots as mixture begins to thicken. When boiling, remove from heat.

Recipe makes 4 servings.

Each serving provides:

80	Calories	0.3 g	Fat
2 g	Protein	0.04 g	Saturated fat
18.3 g	Carbohydrate	0 mg	Cholesterol

Diabetic exchanges: Vegetable, 2; fruit, ½

Oriental Cucumbers

Here's an exotic way to prepare the humble cucumber. You'll be delighted by the flavors. Before serving, sprinkle toasted sesame seeds over cucumbers.

2 cucumbers, peeled and seeded
3 tablespoons rice vinegar
3 packets Equal sweetener
1 teaspoon dark sesame oil*
1 tablespoon soy sauce
¼ teaspoon salt

Slice cucumbers and place in medium bowl. Combine vinegar, sweetener, oil, soy sauce, and salt, whisking to mix, and pour over cucumbers. Cover and allow to marinate in refrigerator several hours before serving.

Recipe makes 6 servings.

Each serving provides:

24	Calories	0.9 g	Fat
1.2 g	Protein	0.15 g	Saturated fat
3.2 g	Carbohydrate	0 mg	Cholesterol

Diabetic exchange: Vegetable, 1

---

*This can be found in the Asian foods section of the market.

Green Beans with Roasted Onions

Try this twist on green beans. Bet you'll love it.

Nonstick butter-flavored cooking spray
1 small to medium onion, chopped
$^{1}/_{2}$ cup concentrated Campbell's 98-percent fat-free cream
    of mushroom soup
2 tablespoons fat-free sour cream
$^{1}/_{2}$ teaspoon Molly McButter dry butter flavor sprinkles*
$^{1}/_{2}$ teaspoon dry onion flakes
Black pepper to taste
$^{1}/_{3}$ cup skim milk
1 can (14 ounces) French-cut green beans, drained
$^{1}/_{3}$ cup crunchy Chinese noodles

*This can be found in small bottles in the baking supplies section of the market.

Preheat oven to 350 degrees F

Spray skillet with nonstick cooking spray and add chopped onion. Brown onions to a deep brown. Be careful, these burn easily.

In a medium bowl, mix together soup, sour cream, butter flavor sprinkles, dry onion flakes, pepper, and skim milk. Whisk if necessary to smooth. Add drained green beans to this mixture and stir gently.

Spray medium casserole dish with nonstick cooking spray. Pour green bean mixture into dish and sprinkle top with crispy noodles. Bake in 350 degree F oven for 20 to 25 minutes.

Recipe makes 6 servings.

Each serving provides:

48	Calories	1.4 g	Fat
1.8 g	Protein	0.32 g	Saturated fat
7.6 g	Carbohydrate	1 mg	Cholesterol

Diabetic exchanges: Starch, ¹/₂; vegetable, ¹/₃

Crunchy Pea Salad

—✾—

This salad is a real treat! Filled with crunch and flavor, it's bound to become a favorite.

2 cups frozen green peas, thawed
$^1/_3$ cup chopped red onion
$^1/_3$ cup chopped celery
3 tablespoons fat-free mayonnaise
3 tablespoons fat-free Miracle Whip
$^1/_3$ cup fat-free shredded Cheddar cheese
$^1/_4$ cup roasted peanuts

In large bowl, combine all ingredients and mix well. Serve chilled or at room temperature.

Recipe makes 4 servings.

Each serving provides:

164	Calories	3.7 g	Fat
12.3 g	Protein	0.98 g	Saturated fat
21.4 g	Carbohydrate	3 mg	Cholesterol

Diabetic exchanges: Vegetable, 3; lean meat, 1; fat, $^3/_4$

Sweet and Sour Rice Salad

———— ✽ ————

This is wonderful during the summer, when you just can't imagine having anything hot on the table.

3 cups cooked rice
1 cup corn (frozen or fresh)
1 can (15 ounces) black beans, drained and rinsed
$^1/_2$ red bell pepper, chopped
$^1/_2$ green bell pepper, chopped
1 red onion, chopped
1 cup pineapple tidbits
2 tablespoons Equal sweetener
2 tablespoons canola oil
$^2/_3$ cup rice vinegar
Salt

In large mixing bowl, combine rice, corn, beans, red and green peppers, onion, and pineapple. In smaller bowl, whisk together sweetener, oil, and vinegar, then pour over rice mixture. Add salt to taste. Cover and chill several hours, even overnight, before serving.

Recipe makes 6 servings. One serving equals 1 cup.

Each serving provides:

218	Calories	4 g	Fat
8.2 g	Protein	0.37 g	Saturated fat
37.7 g	Carbohydrate	0 mg	Cholesterol

Diabetic exchanges: Starch, 1; vegetable, 2;
lean protein, 1; fat, $^3/_4$

Salsa Salad

This salad could also be served as a dip with tortilla chips. It has a delightful bite!

1 can (11 ounces) white shoe peg corn (or other white corn), drained
½ green bell pepper, chopped
½ red bell pepper, chopped
1 small to medium red onion, chopped
2 small tomatoes, chopped
1 cucumber, peeled and chopped
1 jalapeño (or about 1 tablespoon), chopped
2 to 3 tablespoons fresh chopped cilantro
Juice of 1 lime
Garlic salt
Seasoned salt
Pepper

In large bowl, combine all ingredients and mix well, using garlic salt, seasoned salt, and pepper to taste. Cover and refrigerate until chilled.

Recipe makes 6 servings. One serving equals ½ cup.

Each serving provides:

60	Calories	0.6 g	Fat
2.1 g	Protein	0.1 g	Saturated fat
13.8 g	Carbohydrate	0 mg	Cholesterol

Diabetic exchanges: Vegetable, 2; fruit, ⅙

Santa Fe Soup

—❦—

Southwest flavor at it's best! Great served with baked tortilla chips.

Nonfat nonstick cooking spray
2 slices turkey bacon, cut into small pieces
1 medium onion, chopped
1 can (14 ounces) fat-free chicken broth
1 can (16 ounces) golden hominy, drained
1 can (4 ounces) chopped green chilies
2 cups water
1 clove garlic, pressed
$^1/_2$ cup fat-free sour cream
Black pepper

Spray medium saucepan with cooking spray. Brown bacon pieces and onion. Add chicken broth, hominy, chilies, water, and garlic, and simmer over medium to low heat for 15 to 20 minutes. Just before serving, stir in sour cream with whisk and add black pepper to taste.

Recipe makes 6 servings.

Each serving provides:

67	Calories	1 g	Fat
3.7 g	Protein	0.17 g	Saturated fat
11 g	Carbohydrate	3 mg	Cholesterol

Diabetic exchanges: Starch, $^1/_4$; vegetable, 1; fat, $^1/_2$

Spicy Peanut Chicken Salad

—✤—

Wow! This is one of those dishes that, when you serve it, everyone wants the recipe. It is out of this world!

Salad
1 tablespoon rice vinegar
1 large head iceberg lettuce, shredded
1 large cucumber, peeled and chopped
4 green onions, chopped
2 cups cooked, shredded, or chopped chicken breast

Dressing
$1/2$ cup peanut butter
1 tablespoon rice vinegar
6 packets Equal sweetener
2 teaspoons dark sesame oil*
4 tablespoons soy sauce
6 tablespoons chicken broth
$1/8$ to $1/4$ teaspoon cayenne (red) pepper

*This can be found in the Asian foods section of the market.

Sprinkle rice vinegar over lettuce, cucumber, and green onion, and mix well. Arrange in bottom of 9 × 13-inch serving dish. Distribute chicken evenly over lettuce. In medium bowl, blend peanut butter, vinegar, sweetener, oil, soy sauce, chicken broth, and cayenne pepper, and drizzle over chicken and lettuce. Serve immediately.

Recipe makes 8 servings.

Each serving provides:

198	Calories	10.8 g	Fat
19 g	Protein	2.14 g	Saturated fat
7.2 g	Carbohydrate	35 mg	Cholesterol

Diabetic exchanges: Vegetable, 2; lean meat, 2

Sauerkraut Salad

—◆—

Yum!

¹/₂ cup vinegar
12 packets Equal sweetener
1 can (14¹/₂ ounces) sauerkraut, drained
1 small red onion, chopped
¹/₂ cup chopped celery
¹/₂ cup chopped green bell pepper
¹/₂ cup chopped red bell pepper
Salt and pepper, optional

Heat vinegar in small pan. Add sweetener, stirring to dissolve, then let cool. In large mixing bowl, combine sauerkraut, onion, celery, green and red peppers, and optional salt and pepper. Pour cooled vinegar mixture over all. Mix well, cover, and chill in refrigerator overnight.

Recipe makes 12 servings.

Each serving provides:			
19	Calories	0.1 g	Fat
1.5 g	Protein	0.02 g	Saturated fat
3.7 g	Carbohydrate	0 mg	Cholesterol

Diabetic exchange: Vegetable, 1

Summer Cucumber Salad

—❦—

Sounds strange. . . . Tastes great!

2 small cucumbers, grated
1 box (0.3 ounces) sugar-free lemon Jell-O
½ cup very hot water
1 small onion, finely chopped
½ cup fat-free mayonnaise
1 tablespoon vinegar
1 cup 1-percent lowfat cottage cheese

Blot grated cucumbers well on paper towel. In large serving bowl, dissolve lemon Jell-O in hot water. Add onion, mayonnaise, vinegar, cottage cheese, and cucumbers, mixing well. Chill several hours before serving.

Recipe makes 6 servings.

Each serving provides:

63	Calories	0.5 g	Fat
6.1 g	Protein	0.26 g	Saturated fat
8.5 g	Carbohydrate	2 mg	Cholesterol

Diabetic exchanges: Vegetable, 1; skim milk, ²/₅

Veggie Pockets

Sort of like an eggroll.

1 ½ cups shredded carrots
1 ½ cups shredded cabbage
1 small onion, chopped
½ cup fat-free chicken broth
1 tablespoon Molly McButter dry butter flavor sprinkles*
Black pepper
Nonfat nonstick butter-flavored cooking spray
4 eggroll wrappers**

Preheat oven to 400 degrees F

In medium saucepan, combine carrots, cabbage, onion, chicken broth, butter flavor sprinkles, and black pepper to taste. Cover and simmer over medium heat for 5 minutes. Remove lid and cook another 5 minutes or until almost all liquid is gone.

Spray baking sheet with cooking spray. Using large dinner plate as work surface for eggroll wrappers, place one wrapper on plate and one-fourth of vegetable mixture

*This can be found in small bottles in the baking supplies section of the market.

**Usually found in the produce section of the market.

in center of wrapper. Fold one corner of wrapper up and over veggies. Fold opposite corner over, and repeat for remaining corners, like wrapping a small package. Use a drop of water to seal final flap. Place flap-side-up on baking sheet. Repeat procedure for remaining wrappers.

After all rolls are placed on baking sheet, spray tops with cooking spray and bake at 400 degrees F for 14 minutes.

Recipe makes 4 servings.

Each serving provides:

123	Calories	0.3 g	Fat
4.3 g	Protein	0.03 g	Saturated fat
26.6 g	Carbohydrate	0 mg	Cholesterol

Diabetic exchanges: Vegetable, 2; starch, 1

Oriental Peanut Salad

———— ❦ ————

None better—awesome blend of flavors!

4 ounces dry fettuccini or linguini noodles
2½ tablespoons soy sauce
¼ teaspoon sesame oil
1 teaspoon rice vinegar
¼ teaspoon minced fresh ginger
¼ cup grated carrot
1 tablespoon fresh cilantro, chopped
1½ tablespoons chopped peanuts

Cook pasta in boiling water until almost done (al dente).
Rinse in cold water.

Mix together soy sauce, sesame oil, rice vinegar,
and fresh ginger. Stir in noodles, tossing to coat. Add
carrot, cilantro, and peanuts. Toss to coat. Serve at room
temperature.

Recipe makes 2 servings.

Each serving provides:

273	Calories	5.0 g	Fat
10.2 g	Protein	0.69 g	Saturated fat
47.3 g	Carbohydrate	0 mg	Cholesterol

Diabetic exchanges: Starch, 2¾; vegetable, ¼ ; fat, 1

Santa Fe Salad

———✂———

Lively colors and flavors!

3 cups fresh chopped iceberg lettuce
1 fresh green chile pepper (mild), sliced
$1/2$ cup canned brown or Mexican beans, drained
$1/2$ cup chopped onion
1 cup fresh chopped spinach
$1/4$ cup fresh chopped parsley
1 cup fresh chopped tomato
$1/4$ fresh bell pepper, chopped, I like red or yellow
Salad dressing to taste

Toss all ingredients for salad in large bowl. Store salad in fridge until ready to serve. After chilling add dressing of choice. Toss and serve.

Recipe makes 4 servings.

Each serving provides:

60	Calories	0.5 g	Fat
3.4 g	Protein	0.04 g	Saturated fat
11.3 g	Carbohydrate	0 mg	Cholesterol

Diabetic exchanges: Starch, $1/3$; vegetable, $1 1/2$

Sweet and Sour Cabbage

—❧—

This recipe gives the lowly cabbage an exotic flare.

Nonfat nonstick cooking spray
4 cups shredded cabbage
$1/2$ teaspoon salt
3 tablespoons rice vinegar
4 to 5 packets Equal sweetener
1 tablespoon soy sauce

Spray large skillet or wok with cooking spray. Mix all ingredients together in skillet or wok. Cover and cook over medium-low heat 10 minutes, stirring often.

Recipe makes 6 servings.

Each serving provides:

16	Calories	0.2 g	Fat
1.4 g	Protein	0.01 g	Saturated fat
2.9 g	Carbohydrate	0 mg	Cholesterol

Diabetic exchange: Vegetable, 1

Pasta Veggie Sauce

———— ❦ ————

This is one of our favorites, colorful and packed with flavor. Serve this sauce over your favorite hot pasta.

1 medium onion, chopped
1 tablespoon olive oil
3 large cloves garlic, pressed
1 cup marsala
1 cup chopped broccoli
$^1/_2$ cup chopped zucchini
$^1/_2$ cup chopped crookneck yellow squash
1 cup chopped fresh mushrooms
1 large tomato, cubed
$^1/_2$ cup liquid Butter Buds butter flavor granules, prepared
    according to package
Salt

Sauté onion in olive oil in large skillet over medium heat, 1 to 2 minutes. Add garlic and marsala. Reduce heat to low and simmer uncovered for 5 minutes. Add broccoli, zucchini, crookneck squash, and mushrooms. Stir and cover; simmer over low heat for 5 minutes. Add tomato and liquid Butter Buds and stir. Add salt to taste.

Recipe makes 4 servings.

	Each serving provides:		
104	Calories	3.9 g	Fat
2.4 g	Protein	0.60 g	Saturated fat
15.0 g	Carbohydrate	0 mg	Cholesterol

Diabetic exchanges: Vegetable, 3; fat, $^1/_2$

Southern Potato Salad

—❧—

Good old-fashioned flavor. Bring it on a picnic.

1 large potato, boiled, peeled, and chopped
2 green onions, chopped
2 hard-boiled eggs, peeled and yolks discarded, chop
     egg whites only
1 tablespoon chopped dill pickle
1 tablespoon chopped sweet pickle
1 stalk celery, chopped
1/4 teaspoon dill weed
Salt and black pepper to taste
1/3 cup fat-free mayonnaise
1 teaspoon prepared mustard
1 tablespoon fat-free sour cream

In medium bowl, combine potato, green onions, egg whites, chopped pickles, celery, dill weed, salt, and pepper. Mix with spoon.
     In small bowl, combine mayonnaise, mustard, and sour cream. Pour mayonnaise and mustard mixture over potato mixture and stir gently. Chill before serving.

Recipe makes 3 servings.

Each serving provides:

115	Calories	0.2 g	Fat
4.5 g	Protein	0.03 g	Saturated fat
23.4 g	Carbohydrate	0 mg	Cholesterol

Diabetic exchanges: Starch, 1 1/8; lean meat, 1/4; vegetable, 1/2

Restaurant-Style Potato Skins

Out of this world!

2 medium baking potatoes
³/₄ cup fat-free sour cream
2 green onions, chopped
2 slices turkey bacon, cooked and crushed
Nonstick butter-flavored cooking spray
¹/₃ cup Sargento light grated Cheddar cheese

Preheat oven to 400 degrees F

Bake potatoes about 1 hour at 400 degrees F. Remove from oven and allow to cool enough to handle. Slice each potato in half lengthwise and scoop out some of the center of each half to make room for filling. Combine sour cream, onion, and bacon. Fill potato halves.

Spray a baking dish or pan with nonstick cooking spray and place filled potatoes in dish to bake. Save grated cheese for topping. Bake in 400 degree F oven for 10 to 12 minutes. Remove and serve.

Recipe makes 4 servings.

Each serving provides:

150	Calories	2.3 g	Fat
8.7 g	Protein	1.37 g	Saturated fat
24.4 g	Carbohydrate	8 mg	Cholesterol

Diabetic exchanges: Starch, 1¹/₄; lean meat, 1

Orange Crispy Sweet Potatoes

A great way for kids or adults to enjoy something that's good for them.

Nonfat nonstick cooking spray
1 medium sweet potato, peeled and sliced ¼ inch thick
3 tablespoons frozen orange juice concentrate, thawed
1 cup crushed cornflakes
Seasoned salt, optional

Preheat oven to 375 degrees F

Spray medium baking sheet with cooking spray. Place sliced sweet potatoes in small bowl and drizzle orange juice over all slices. Toss to make sure all slices are exposed to orange juice. Pour sweet potatoes into a plastic bag and add crushed cornflakes. Toss gently. Place coated potatoes on baking sheet. Bake at 375 degrees F for 20 minutes. Sprinkle with seasoned salt, if desired.

Recipe makes 4 servings.

Each serving provides:

147	Calories	0.2 g	Fat
2.7 g	Protein	0.02 g	Saturated fat
34.9 g	Carbohydrate	0 mg	Cholesterol

Diabetic exchanges: Starch, 1½; fruit, ½

Fresh Vegetable Medley

———❧———

This is the Grand Champion of all squash recipes!

Nonfat nonstick cooking spray
1/2 cup chopped onion
1 yellow crookneck squash, chopped
1 zucchini
4 small Roma tomatoes, chopped
1 tablespoon fresh basil, chopped
1 teaspoon garlic salt

Spray large skillet with cooking spray. Over medium heat, sauté onion, stirring often, for several minutes or until translucent. Add crookneck squash, zucchini, tomatoes, basil, and garlic salt, and reduce heat to low. Cover and simmer 5 to 10 minutes or until squash is tender (not mushy!).

Recipe makes 4 servings.

Each serving provides:

34	Calories	0.5 g	Fat
1.5 g	Protein	0.06 g	Saturated fat
7.2 g	Carbohydrate	0 mg	Cholesterol

Diabetic exchange: Vegetable, 1 1/2

Main Dishes and Casseroles

Beef and Bean Ranch Bake
Beef and Potato Pie
Beef Stroganoff
German Meat and Cabbage Pie
Blackened Burgers
Chuckwagon Cheeseburgers
Breakfast Casserole
Buttery Rice Bake
Baked Cheese Pie
Alice's Best Chili
Chicken and Dressing Casserole
Chicken-Fried Chicken with Cream Gravy
Chicken with Roasted Vegetables and Garlic
Chili Corn Bake
Creamed Tuna on Toast
Curried Apricot Chicken
Crispy Chicken with Cheese
Dijon Baked Chicken
Cheesy Breakfast Eggs
Fried Rice

Ultra Lowfat Lasagna
Overnight French Toast Casserole
Luncheon Chicken Salad
Macaroni and Cheese
Old-Fashioned Meatloaf
Mexican Chicken and Noodles
Orange Beef and Vegetable Stir Fry
Paprika Chicken
Pasta Primavera
Italian Pasta and Vegetables
Pepperoni Pizza Rolls
Pepper Steak
Pizza Rolls
Pepperoni Mini Pizzas
Our Favorite Pizza Crust
Pork Tenders in Gravy
Spicy Noodles
Rice Pilaf
Hearty Ranch Biscuit Bake
Hearty Skillet Breakfast
Chicken Sour Cream Enchiladas
Old-Fashioned Beef Stew
Sweet Spicy Chicken Breasts
Taco Rolls
Homestyle Skillet Stew
Tender Smothered Pork and Potatoes

Vegetarian Enchiladas
Grilled Italian Veggie Sandwich
Potluck Casserole
Grilled Vegetables with Chicken
Layered Potato Bake
Asian Peanut Chicken on Rice
Breakfast Sausage Gravy and Biscuits
Tomato and Basil Pasta
Buttermilk Chicken
Cheese Bake with Spinach
Honey Dijon Baked Crispy Chicken
Chicken Breasts with Lemon Sauce
Chicken Breasts with Pimiento Sauce
Family Casserole
Honey Mustard Chicken
Orange-Almond Chicken
Spicy Garlic Butter Shrimp
Southwest White Chili
Spicy Jalapeño Chicken Breasts
Tex-Mex Burrito
Avocado and Cream Cheese Sandwich
Pepper Chicken
The Best Tortilla Casserole
Sour Cream Veggie Enchiladas
Veggie Quiche

Beef and Bean Ranch Bake

—❧—

Wow, is this casserole terrific! Something about it makes you want to go find your old cowboy hat and wear it while you eat. Come to think of it, leftovers (if there are any) would travel nicely in a Roy Rogers and Dale Evans lunch box.

1 pound lean ground beef
1 medium onion, chopped
1 can (10¾ ounces) Healthy Choice cream of
    mushroom soup
1 can (15 ounces) ranch-style beans
1 package (1 pound) grated fat-free Cheddar cheese
Salt and black pepper, optional
Nonfat nonstick cooking spray
1 package (1 pound) grated hash brown potatoes (fresh
    or frozen)

Preheat oven to 350 degrees F

In large skillet, sauté beef and onion until done; drain any grease. Add mushroom soup, beans, and cheese. Season with salt and black pepper, if desired, stirring well. Spray 9 × 13-inch casserole dish with cooking spray. Distribute hash browns over bottom of casserole dish and spread meat mixture on top. Bake uncovered at 350 degrees F for 25 minutes.

Recipe makes 6 to 8 servings.

Each serving provides:

304	Calories	8.4 g	Fat
30.4 g	Protein	4.33 g	Saturated fat
25.0 g	Carbohydrate	40 mg	Cholesterol

Diabetic exchanges: Starch, 1; medium fat protein, 2; vegetable, 1; skim milk, ½

Beef and Potato Pie

———❦———

This might be considered a sneaky way to get meat-and-potato people to eat their vegetables. Delicious and easy to prepare, this will soon become a favorite.

Meat Pie
Nonfat nonstick cooking spray
1 pound lean ground beef
1/4 teaspoon onion powder
1/4 teaspoon garlic powder
1 teaspoon Worcestershire sauce
1/3 cup rolled oats
1/4 cup fat-free liquid egg product
1 can (8 ounces) tomato sauce
1 cup frozen mixed vegetables
Salt and black pepper

Potato Topping
3 large potatoes, cubed and boiled
2 tablespoons Molly McButter dry butter flavor sprinkles*
1/4 cup evaporated skim milk
1/2 cup light Cheddar cheese

*This can be found in small bottles in the baking supplies section of the market.

Preheat oven to 350 degrees F

Spray 8- or 9-inch pie plate with cooking spray. Combine beef, onion powder, garlic powder, Worcestershire sauce, oats, egg product, tomato sauce, mixed vegetables, and salt and black pepper (if desired). Mix well. Press mixture into pie plate and bake at 350 degrees F for 30 minutes.

Mash potatoes with butter flavor sprinkles, milk, and cheese. When beef dish has baked 30 minutes, remove, spread potato topping over meat, and return to bake another 10 minutes at 350 degrees F. Cut into wedges to serve.

Recipe makes 4 to 6 servings.

Each serving provides:

331	Calories	15.1 g	Fat
21.7 g	Protein	6.35 g	Saturated fat
26.3 g	Carbohydrate	59 mg	Cholesterol

Diabetic exchanges: Starch, 1; medium protein, 2; vegetable, 2; skim milk, 1/2

Beef Stroganoff

Great for special dinners . . . or when you just want to
treat yourself extra special.

Nonfat nonstick cooking spray
½ pound thin-sliced, fajita-style beef strips
⅓ cup flour
Salt and black pepper
1 medium onion, chopped
1 can (14½ ounces) fat-free chicken broth
1½ cups fat-free sour cream
1 tablespoon Molly McButter dry butter flavor sprinkles*
1 teaspoon Worcestershire sauce
1 package (1 ounce) powdered ranch dressing mix
3 cups fresh sliced mushrooms
1 package (12 ounces) No Yolk noodles, cooked

Spray large skillet with cooking spray. Dust beef strips
with flour and place in skillet. Season, as desired, with salt
and black pepper, and brown on both sides over medium-
high heat. Lower heat and add onion. Continue to cook
over low heat for about 5 minutes.

*This can be found in small bottles in the baking supplies section of the market.

In medium bowl, combine chicken broth, sour cream, butter flavor sprinkles, Worcestershire sauce, and dressing mix. Whisk or stir until well blended. Stir in mushrooms and add mixture to meat and onions in skillet. Simmer until mushrooms are done, 15 to 20 minutes. Serve over cooked noodles.

Recipe makes 4 servings. One serving equals approximately ³/₄ cup.

Each serving provides:

573	Calories	9.2 g	Fat
38.6 g	Protein	3.08 g	Saturated fat
82.0 g	Carbohydrate	39 mg	Cholesterol

Diabetic exchanges: Starch, 4; medium protein, 3; vegetable, 1

German Meat and Cabbage Pie

———❧———

Frozen pie crusts make this hearty meal a snap to prepare. If you like German *bierocks*, you'll love this!

1 pound lean ground beef
1 large onion, chopped
3 cups chopped or shredded cabbage
2 tablespoons Molly McButter dry butter flavor sprinkles*
Salt and black pepper
Nonfat nonstick cooking spray
2 (8-inch) frozen pie crusts, thawed

Preheat oven to 350 degrees F

In large skillet, brown beef and onion over medium heat. Add cabbage, butter flavor sprinkles, and desired amount of salt and black pepper. Reduce heat and cover skillet. Simmer 30 minutes.

*This can be found in small bottles in the baking supplies section of the market.

Spray cookie sheet with cooking spray. Remove pie crusts from tins and place one crust on sheet. Spoon meat and cabbage mixture into pie crust, up to about ½- to 1-inch from rim. Cover meat mixture with second pie crust. Gently pinch the edges of the two crusts together to seal pie. If a browner crust is desired, brush top of pie with milk. Bake at 350 degrees F for 30 minutes, until golden. Cut into wedges to serve.

Recipe makes 6 servings.

Each serving provides:

386	Calories	20.2 g	Fat
17.9 g	Protein	7.67 g	Saturated fat
29.2 g	Carbohydrate	56 mg	Cholesterol

Diabetic exchanges: Starch, 2; vegetable, 2; lean meat, 2; fat, 1½

Blackened Burgers

———— ❦ ————

For those who like their burgers to have a delicious zing.
Serve on bun with lettuce, tomato, mustard, and other
burger favorites. Enjoy!

Nonfat nonstick cooking spray
1 pound ground turkey breast
2 tablespoons fat-free liquid egg product
1 tablespoon dry onion flakes
1/4 cup rolled oats
1/3 cup tomato sauce
1 clove garlic, pressed
2 tablespoons A.1. steak sauce
2 teaspoons blackened spices* (additional for sprinkling
    on outsides of burgers)

*We like Chef Paul Prudhomme's Blackened Steak Magic.

Spray large skillet with cooking spray. In large bowl, combine turkey, egg product, onion flakes, oats, tomato sauce, garlic, A.1. steak sauce, and spices. Mix with large spoon until thoroughly blended. Form meat mixture into six patties. Sprinkle both sides of each patty with blackened spices and place in skillet. Brown on both sides over medium-high heat, then lower heat and cover part of the time to steam and cook thoroughly.

Recipe makes 6 servings.

Each serving provides:

112	Calories	1.5 g	Fat
16.8 g	Protein	0.39 g	Saturated fat
7.0 g	Carbohydrate	38 mg	Cholesterol

Diabetic exchange: lean protein, 2

Chuckwagon Cheeseburgers

———— ✧ ————

We are both from the greasy-burger era of the 1950s and occasionally long for that old taste. These burgers satisfy that craving.

Nonfat nonstick cooking spray
1 pound extra lean ground beef
2 tablespoons Lipton's onion soup mix (dry)
$\frac{1}{8}$ teaspoon liquid smoke
$\frac{1}{2}$ cup Kraft grated fat-free cheese
2 tablespoons fat-free liquid egg product
2 tablespoons Campbell's 98-percent fat-free cream of
    mushroom soup*
Black pepper

Spray skillet with cooking spray. Combine beef, onion soup mix, liquid smoke, cheese, egg product, mushroom soup, and black pepper (as desired), in medium bowl and mix thoroughly. Form meat mixture into six patties. In

*Omit the cream of mushroom soup if you prefer to cook these outdoors on the grill. As with any ground beef, be sure to cook thoroughly.

skillet on somewhat low heat, brown patties on one side. Because fat-free cheese tends to stick, cook thoroughly on one side then turn gently and brown on the other side.

Recipe makes 6 servings.

Each serving provides:

159	Calories	9.8 g	Fat
14.3 g	Protein	4.04 g	Saturated fat
2.8 g	Carbohydrate	40 mg	Cholesterol

Diabetic exchange: Lean protein, 3

Breakfast Casserole

———— ✣ ————

A breakfast that can be prepared the night before. . . .
What a great idea! Especially if you are "morning-
challenged," as we prefer to call it.

Nonfat nonstick butter-flavored cooking spray
2 slices white bread, cut into small cubes
1 cup grated fat-free Cheddar cheese
1 cup fat-free liquid egg product
1 cup skim milk
1/8 teaspoon onion powder
Pepper
Salt, optional

Preheat oven to 325 degrees F

Spray 8-inch casserole dish with cooking spray. In
medium bowl, combine bread, cheese, egg product, milk,
and onion powder. Add pepper, to taste, and salt if desired. Pour into casserole dish. Cover and refrigerate
overnight.

Remove cover from casserole and bake at 325
degrees F for 35 to 40 minutes, until set.

Recipe makes 4 servings.

Each serving provides:

119	Calories	0.7 g	Fat
17.1 g	Protein	0.77 g	Saturated fat
10.8 g	Carbohydrate	6 mg	Cholesterol

Diabetic exchanges: Starch, 1; skim milk, 1/2

Buttery Rice Bake

———— ✦ ————

This delicious rice dish is so easy. It has a delicate flavor that goes well with just about anything you serve. If you are feeding people who say "yuck" to mushrooms, just omit them. (The mushrooms, not the people!)

Nonfat nonstick cooking spray
1 cup uncooked white rice
1 jar (4 ounces) sliced mushrooms
½ cup Butter Buds (prepared according to package directions)
¼ cup white cooking wine
1 can (14½ ounces) fat-free chicken broth
Salt

Preheat oven to 350 degrees F

Spray 2-quart casserole dish with cooking spray. In large bowl, combine rice, mushrooms, Butter Buds, wine, and chicken broth. Season with salt and pour mixture into casserole dish. Cover with lid or aluminum foil. Bake at 350 degrees F for 50 minutes.

Recipe makes 3 to 4 servings.

Each serving provides:

199	Calories	0.6 g	Fat
4.9 g	Protein	0.18 g	Saturated fat
42.3 g	Carbohydrate	0 mg	Cholesterol

Diabetic exchanges: Starch, 2; vegetable, 1

Baked Cheese Pie

—❧—

Marvelous, savory flavor! This brings back memories of the days when all the really trendy people sat around eating quiche. If you still want to be trendy, add a bit of fresh basil to it . . . and then go out and have a latte.

Nonfat nonstick cooking spray
1 (9-inch) frozen pie crust*
1 carton (24 ounces) fat-free cottage cheese, drained
½ cup fat-free liquid egg product
1 bunch green onions, chopped
¼ cup chopped green bell pepper
1 clove fresh garlic, pressed
4 slices Kraft fat-free American cheese
4 slices Kraft fat-free mozzarella cheese
2 tablespoons Parmesan cheese
Black pepper

Preheat oven to 350 degrees F

Spray 9-inch glass pie plate with cooking spray. Remove pie crust from tin while frozen and place in glass pie plate. Let stand for 10 to 15 minutes to thaw, and then gently mold and press the crust to fit the plate.

*We like Pillsbury Pet Ritz (4 grams of fat per serving).

In large bowl, combine cottage cheese, egg product, onions, green pepper, and garlic. Stir to mix thoroughly. Pour about one third of mixture into unbaked pie shell. Top with 4 slices of American cheese. Pour in another one third of mixture and cover with 4 mozzarella cheese slices. Pour remaining one third of mixture on top. Sprinkle with Parmesan cheese and black pepper, to taste. Bake at 350 degrees F for 1 hour. Remove and cool slightly. Serve warm.

Recipe makes 8 servings.

Each serving provides:

184	Calories	4.4 g	Fat
20.4 g	Protein	1.74 g	Saturated fat
15.2 g	Carbohydrate	10 mg	Cholesterol

Diabetic exchanges: Vegetable, 1½; lean protein, 3

Alice's Best Chili

—❦—

When winter weather is forecast, we head to the store for ingredients to make this chili. It *must* be a scientific fact that a hot bowl of chili on a cold night makes everything okay. Actually, this chili's even better when made the day before; so stay on top of that weather forecast!

Nonfat nonstick cooking spray
1 pound lean ground beef
$1/2$ cup chopped onion
$1/3$ cup ketchup
$1/4$ cup water
$1/4$ cup chopped celery
1 tablespoon lemon juice
2 teaspoons brown sugar
1 teaspoon Worcestershire sauce
$1/2$ teaspoon salt
$1/2$ teaspoon vinegar
$1/8$ teaspoon dry mustard
$1 1/2$ cups cooked pinto beans
$1 1/2$ cups tomato juice
$1 1/2$ tablespoons chili powder

Spray large saucepan with cooking spray. Lightly brown beef and onion. Drain any grease from pan. Add ketchup, water, celery, lemon juice, brown sugar, Worcestershire sauce, salt, vinegar, and mustard. Cover pan and simmer over low heat for 30 minutes. Add beans, tomato juice, and chili powder. It's ready to serve when thoroughly heated.

Recipe makes 4 to 6 servings.

Each serving provides:

293	Calories	10.4 g	Fat
18.5 g	Protein	3.88 g	Saturated fat
32.5 g	Carbohydrate	38 mg	Cholesterol

Diabetic exchanges: Vegetable, 3; medium protein, 3

Chicken and Dressing Casserole

Delicious chicken and dressing the easy way! The aroma of this dish as it bakes is heavenly. It brings back memories of long ago Sunday dinners when there must have been a law that made everyone serve chicken.

3 boneless, skinless chicken breasts (3 ounces each)
3 cups fat-free chicken broth
1/4 cup flour
1 tablespoon Molly McButter dry butter flavor sprinkles*
1/2 cup fat-free liquid egg product
Nonfat nonstick cooking spray
1 1/2 cups dressing mix
Salt and black pepper

Preheat oven to 350 degrees F

Cook chicken breasts and broth in medium saucepan, simmering 35 to 45 minutes. Saving broth to use in casserole, drain and set chicken aside to cool.

Measure flour into saucepan. Using a whisk, slowly mix chicken broth into flour over medium heat. Add butter flavor sprinkles and continue whisking until thickened. Add egg product and continue stirring and cooking 2 to 3 minutes more.

*This can be found in small bottles in the baking supplies section of the market.

To assemble casserole, spray 9 × 13-inch casserole dish with cooking spray. Shred or chop chicken into small pieces and cover bottom of casserole dish with chicken pieces. Top with dry dressing. Add salt and pepper to taste. Pour hot broth mixture over top. Cover and bake at 350 degrees F for 30 minutes.

Recipe makes 4 to 6 servings.

Each serving provides:

108	Calories	1.0 g	Fat
13.6 g	Protein	0.25 g	Saturated fat
9.7 g	Carbohydrate	24 mg	Cholesterol

Diabetic exchanges: Lean protein, 1½; starch, ½

Chicken-Fried Chicken with Cream Gravy

Out of this world. . . . Doris's personal favorite!

Chicken
Nonfat nonstick cooking spray
4 boneless, skinless chicken breasts (3 ounces each)
2 egg whites, slightly beaten
2 cups crushed cornflakes
Salt and black pepper, optional

Gravy
4 tablespoons flour
1 cup fat-free chicken broth
1/2 cup evaporated skim milk
1 cup skim milk
2 teaspoons Molly McButter dry butter flavor sprinkles*
Salt and black pepper, optional

Spray large skillet with cooking spray. Lightly pound each chicken breast until thin and tenderized, then dip in egg whites and roll in cornflakes. Place chicken in skillet and brown slowly, turning only once, over *low* heat because they burn easily over higher heat. Remove from skillet when thoroughly cooked and sprinkle with salt and pepper, if desired. Add flour to skillet and brown over medium heat, stirring occasionally. This also burns easily, so be vigilant. When flour is browned, remove from heat.

*This can be found in small bottles in the baking supplies section of the market.

In medium bowl, combine chicken broth, evaporated skim milk and regular skim milk, and butter flavor sprinkles. Using a whisk, add to flour in skillet while still removed from heat. Return skillet to medium heat and continue to stir until gravy thickens. Add salt and pepper, if desired. Serve hot gravy over chicken breasts. You will think you have died and gone to heaven!

Recipe makes 4 servings.

Each serving provides:

435	Calories	3.3 g	Fat
38.4 g	Protein	0.99 g	Saturated fat
61.9 g	Carbohydrate	75 mg	Cholesterol

Diabetic exchanges: Lean protein, 4; starch, 2; skim milk, 1/2

Chicken with Roasted Vegetables and Garlic

Wait till you smell this easy, delicious dinner cooking! We love the baked garlic, but you might want to make sure everyone eats at least some of it. Otherwise, they won't want to sit by you.

Nonfat nonstick cooking spray
4 boneless, skinless chicken breasts (3½ ounces each)
⅓ cup flour
1 can (14½ ounces) beef broth, remove fat from top of broth
2 tablespoons rice vinegar
1 teaspoon light soy sauce
1 whole head of garlic, top sliced off to expose cloves
1 package (2½ pounds) fresh-cut stew vegetables*
2 slices turkey bacon, cut into small pieces
½ teaspoon garlic powder
½ teaspoon onion powder
Black pepper

Preheat oven to 350 degrees F

Spray large skillet with cooking spray. Dust chicken breasts on each side with flour and brown in skillet on low heat.

*These can be found in the produce section of the market.

In medium bowl, combine beef broth, rice vinegar, and soy sauce. Spray large baking dish with cooking spray. Arrange browned chicken on bottom of dish. Place head of garlic in center. Arrange cut vegetables and pieces of cut turkey bacon over top of chicken. Pour broth mixture over vegetables and meat. Sprinkle garlic powder, onion powder, and desired amount of black pepper over entire dish. Cover dish with foil or lid and bake at 350 degrees F for 1 hour. Remove cover and bake another 20 minutes.

Recipe makes 4 servings.

Each serving provides:

312	Calories	5.0 g	Fat
33.5 g	Protein	1.24 g	Saturated fat
33.7 g	Carbohydrate	78 mg	Cholesterol

Diabetic exchanges: Lean protein, 4; vegetable, 2; starch, 1/2

Chili Corn Bake

———⚬⚬———

There's nothing boring about this corn dish. Great south-western flavor.

Nonfat nonstick butter-flavored cooking spray
1 can (15 ounces) whole kernel corn, drained
1 can (15 ounces) creamed corn
1 package (8 ounces) light cream cheese, cut into cubes
1 can (4½ ounces) chopped green chilies
1 cup cornflake crumbs

Preheat oven to 300 degrees F

Spray 7 × 11-inch casserole dish with cooking spray. Combine both cans corn and cream cheese cubes in small saucepan. Over low heat, cook and stir until cheese melts. Add chilies with liquid; stir well. Pour into casserole dish and top with cornflake crumbs. Bake at 300 degrees F until lightly browned, about 15 minutes.

Recipe makes 8 servings.

Each serving provides:

186	Calories	6.5 g	Fat
5.7 g	Protein	4.28 g	Saturated fat
29.3 g	Carbohydrate	20 mg	Cholesterol

Diabetic exchanges: Starch, 2; vegetable, 1

Creamed Tuna on Toast

One of us loves this dish with all her heart and considers it a wonderful comfort food. (Hint: Doris hates fish.) The white-sauce base has been de-buttered, and the taste is every bit as good as the old fatty version.

2 tablespoons flour
1 tablespoon Molly McButter dry butter flavor sprinkles*
1 cup canned evaporated skim milk
1 can (6 ounces) water-packed white tuna, drained
Pepper
3 pieces of toast

In a small bowl, whisk together flour, butter flavor sprinkles, and milk. Pour into large skillet and continue whisking over medium heat until thickened. Add tuna, flaking with fork, and distribute it evenly throughout sauce. Remove from heat. Add pepper to taste. To serve, place toast on plates and pour creamed tuna over the toast.

Recipe makes 3 servings.

Each serving provides:

234	Calories	2.5 g	Fat
24.1 g	Protein	0.66 g	Saturated fat
26.2 g	Carbohydrate	27 mg	Cholesterol

Diabetic exchanges: Lean protein, 2; starch, 1; skim milk, 1/2

---

*This can be found in small bottles in the baking supplies section of the market.

Curried Apricot Chicken

If you've never tried anything with curry, you must try this. It's a delicious way to be introduced to this exotic spice. Serve over rice.

Nonfat nonstick cooking spray
4 boneless, skinless chicken breasts ($3\frac{1}{2}$ ounces each)
1 medium onion, chopped
1 to 2 cloves garlic, minced
1 can ($11\frac{1}{2}$ ounces) apricot nectar
2 tablespoons Molly McButter dry butter flavor sprinkles*
2 teaspoons curry powder
1 tablespoon brown sugar substitute

Preheat oven to 350 degrees F

Spray large skillet with cooking spray. Over medium-high heat, brown chicken breasts on both sides. Remove from skillet and set aside. Respray skillet with cooking spray and add onion, stirring over medium heat until tender. Add garlic and stir another minute or so. Add apricot nectar, butter sprinkles, curry powder, and brown sugar substitute, stirring to blend.

*This can be found in small bottles in the baking supplies section of the market.

Spray large casserole dish with cooking spray. Place browned chicken breasts in casserole dish and pour apricot-curry mixture over chicken. Bake at 350 degrees F for 35 to 40 minutes.

Recipe makes 4 servings.

Each serving provides:

225	Calories	3.4 g	Fat
27.7 g	Protein	0.89 g	Saturated fat
18.8 g	Carbohydrate	73 mg	Cholesterol

Diabetic exchanges: Lean protein, 3; fruit, 1

Crispy Chicken with Cheese

———✥———

This is always a big hit.

Nonfat nonstick cooking spray
1 tablespoon lemon juice
$^3/_4$ cup fat-free mayonnaise
$^1/_4$ teaspoon garlic powder
4 boneless, skinless chicken breasts (3 ounces each)
1 cup shredded fat-free Cheddar or American cheese
2 cups crushed cornflakes

Preheat oven to 375 degrees F

Spray large baking sheet with cooking spray. In medium
bowl, mix lemon juice, mayonnaise, and garlic powder
until well blended. Dip chicken breasts first in mayonnaise mixture, then in grated cheese, and last in cornflakes. Be sure each chicken breast is coated well on both
sides. Place on baking sheet. Bake at 375 degrees F until
golden brown, 30 to 35 minutes.

Recipe makes 4 servings.

Each serving provides:

420	Calories	3.1 g	Fat
39.7 g	Protein	1.47 g	Saturated fat
58.4 g	Carbohydrate	78 mg	Cholesterol

Diabetic exchanges: Lean protein, 4; starch, 2$^1/_2$

Dijon Baked Chicken

Easy! Delicious! Lowfat!

Nonfat nonstick cooking spray
$^1/_2$ cup plain nonfat yogurt
$^1/_2$ cup Dijon mustard
4 boneless, skinless chicken breasts (3 ounces each)
1 to 2 cups crushed cornflakes
Salt and black pepper

Preheat oven to 400 degrees F
Spray medium baking sheet with cooking spray. Combine yogurt and mustard in small dish. Dip chicken breasts in mixture to coat, then dip in crushed cornflakes. Sprinkle with salt and pepper, as desired, and place chicken on baking sheet. Bake at 400 degrees F until done, 20 to 30 minutes.

Recipe makes 4 servings.

Each serving provides:

309	Calories	7.1 g	Fat
32.4 g	Protein	0.90 g	Saturated fat
28.3 g	Carbohydrate	74 mg	Cholesterol

Diabetic exchanges: Lean protein, 4; starch, 1

Cheesy Breakfast Eggs

These are lovely, creamy scrambled eggs. Even Alice, who sort of shudders over creamy eggs, loves this. These eggs are also good with salsa.

Nonfat nonstick butter-flavored cooking spray
$^1/_2$ cup fat-free liquid egg product
$^1/_4$ cup 1-percent lowfat cottage cheese
$^1/_4$ cup grated light Cheddar cheese
1 tablespoon Molly McButter dry butter flavor sprinkles*
Pepper

Spray medium skillet with cooking spray. In medium bowl, mix well together egg product, cottage cheese, Cheddar cheese, and butter flavor sprinkles. Pour into skillet and cook over medium heat, turning and stirring often. When eggs are set, add pepper to taste and turn out onto a plate and serve.

Recipe makes 2 servings.

Each serving provides:

98	Calories	2.8 g	Fat
12.5 g	Protein	1.83 g	Saturated fat
3.8 g	Carbohydrate	11 mg	Cholesterol

Diabetic exchange: Lean protein, 1$^3/_4$

---

*This can be found in small bottles in the baking supplies section of the market.

Fried Rice

—❦—

This is a wonderful way to use leftover rice. We especially like to use Japanese sticky rice or jasmine rice in this dish. If you keep leftover rice in a big plastic bag in the refrigerator, it is easy to squeeze the bag to loosen and separate the grains.

3 cups cooked white rice
¼ cup fat-free liquid egg product
2 tablespoons chicken broth
2 teaspoons soy sauce
1 tablespoon peanut oil
2 green onions, chopped
Salt, optional

Loosen rice grains as much as possible to avoid clumps of rice. Mix egg product, chicken broth, and soy sauce together in small bowl. Heat a wok or large skillet over medium-high heat. Add peanut oil and swirl it around. Add green onions, stirring a few times, then add egg mixture. Let stand for only 5 to 10 seconds, then add the rice. Using a spatula, turn and toss continuously until hot, about 3 minutes. Season with salt if desired.

Recipe makes 4 servings. Each serving equals ¾ cup.

Each serving provides:

238	Calories	3.8 g	Fat
5.7 g	Protein	0.70 g	Saturated fat
43.9 g	Carbohydrate	0 mg	Cholesterol

Diabetic exchange: Starch, 3

Ultra Lowfat Lasagna

This is so delicious! Great to freeze and take to work for lunch.

Nonfat nonstick cooking spray
$^1/_2$ pound ground turkey breast
1 jar (26 ounces) lowfat pasta sauce (2 grams of fat or less per $^1/_2$ cup serving)
1 cup sliced fresh mushrooms
3 tablespoons dry onion flakes
2 cloves fresh garlic, pressed
2 teaspoons parsley
$^1/_2$ teaspoon oregano
$^1/_4$ of bell pepper, chopped fine
1 carton (16 ounces) 1-percent cottage cheese
$^1/_2$ cup fat-free liquid egg product
6 oven-ready lasagna noodles*
1 cup grated Kraft fat-free mozzarella cheese
$^3/_4$ cup fat-free sour cream
$^1/_3$ cup fat-free Parmesan cheese
Salt and black pepper, optional

Preheat oven to 350 degrees F

Spray skillet with nonstick cooking spray. Brown ground turkey breast, then add pasta sauce, mushrooms, onion flakes, garlic, parsley, oregano, and bell pepper. Simmer and stir occasionally over low heat for about 10 minutes.

*No boiling required, these can be used right out of the box.

In medium bowl, combine cottage cheese and egg product, and stir.

Spray 11 × 7-inch glass baking dish with cooking spray. Place one layer of oven-ready noodles on the bottom. Add half of meat mixture, then add another layer of noodles. Pour cottage cheese mixture in next. Add a layer of grated fat-free mozzarella cheese and then sour cream. Add another layer of noodles and top those with the remaining meat mixture. Top entire casserole with Parmesan cheese. Sprinkle with salt and pepper, if desired. Bake at 350 degrees F for 1 hour.

Recipe makes 8 servings.

Each serving provides:

266	Calories	3.1 g	Fat
26.4 g	Protein	1.12 g	Saturated fat
32.3 g	Carbohydrate	24 mg	Cholesterol

Diabetic exchanges: Starch, 1½; lean protein, 2; vegetable, 2

Overnight French Toast Casserole

French bread with cinnamon and raisins, yum! Doris thinks it tastes a lot like bread pudding, so perhaps you could also serve it as dessert.

Nonfat nonstick cooking spray
3 slices white bread, cut into small pieces
2 tablespoons Molly McButter dry butter flavor sprinkles*
1 cup fat-free liquid egg product
1 cup skim milk
1 teaspoon vanilla
1 teaspoon cinnamon
¼ cup raisins
2 tablespoons Equal sweetener

Spray 9-inch square baking dish with cooking spray. In large bowl, combine all ingredients, then pour into baking dish. Cover and set in refrigerator for 8 hours or overnight.

When ready to bake, remove dish from refrigerator and heat oven to 350 degrees F. Uncover dish and bake for 30 minutes. Serve with syrup.

Recipe makes 4 servings.

Each serving provides:

160	Calories	0.8 g	Fat
15.0 g	Protein	0.24 g	Saturated fat
21.6 g	Carbohydrate	1 mg	Cholesterol

Diabetic exchanges: Starch, 1; lean protein, 1; skim milk, ¼

*This can be found in small bottles in the baking supplies section of the market.

Luncheon Chicken Salad

This is the most fabulous chicken salad! Alice always thinks about making this on hot summer days, and usually serves it on lettuce leaves. It makes an especially nice luncheon dish if you are trying to impress someone by showing them how refined you are. . . .

4 cups chopped cooked chicken breast
1 cup chopped celery
1 cup halved seedless grapes
$^1\!/_2$ cup fat-free mayonnaise
$^1\!/_4$ cup chopped toasted almonds
$^1\!/_2$ teaspoon lemon juice
Salt and pepper

Combine all ingredients, using salt and pepper to taste. Chill until ready to serve.

Recipe makes 6 servings.

Each serving provides:

223	Calories	6.1 g	Fat
30.5 g	Protein	1.25 g	Saturated fat
10.8 g	Carbohydrate	80 mg	Cholesterol

Diabetic exchanges: Lean meat, 3; vegetable, 1; fruit, $^1\!/_2$

Macaroni and Cheese

Nice and creamy. . . . Down-home flavor!

Macaroni
4 cups cooked macaroni, hot
2 teaspoons Molly McButter dry butter flavor sprinkles*

Sauce
1/2 cup light Velveeta
2 slices Kraft fat-free American cheese
1/2 teaspoon Molly McButter dry butter flavor sprinkles*
1/2 cup skim milk
1/4 cup evaporated skim milk
2 tablespoons fat-free sour cream
Black pepper

Mix cooked, drained, hot macaroni with 2 teaspoons butter flavor sprinkles and stir until sprinkles dissolve. In food processor, combine all sauce ingredients except black pepper and blend until smooth. Pour sauce over macaroni and stir over low heat until thoroughly heated. Add black pepper to taste. Serve and enjoy.

Recipe makes 6 servings. One serving equals approximately 3/4 cup.

Each serving provides:

182	Calories	1.7 g	Fat
9.9 g	Protein	0.78 g	Saturated fat
31.4 g	Carbohydrate	4 mg	Cholesterol

Diabetic exchanges: Starch, 1 1/2; lean meat, 1

---

*This can be found in small bottles in the baking supplies section of the market.

Old-Fashioned Meatloaf

This is a mighty tasty meatloaf and it makes especially good sandwiches the next day.

Nonfat nonstick cooking spray
1 1/2 pounds ground turkey breast
1 can (10 3/4 ounces) Campbell's 98-percent fat-free cream of mushroom soup
2 tablespoons dry onion flakes
1 clove garlic, pressed
1/2 cup fat-free sour cream
1/4 cup fat-free liquid egg product
3/4 cup rolled oats
1 can (6 ounces) tomato paste
Salt and black pepper

Preheat oven to 375 degrees F

Spray 8 1/2 × 4 1/2-inch loaf pan with cooking spray. In large bowl, combine all ingredients, seasoning with salt and pepper, and mix with spoon until thoroughly blended. Press mixture into loaf pan. Bake at 375 degrees F for 1 hour.

Recipe makes 8 servings.

Each serving provides:

181	Calories	2.7 g	Fat
24.2 g	Protein	0.54 g	Saturated fat
14.5 g	Carbohydrate	53 mg	Cholesterol

Diabetic exchanges: Lean meat, 3; vegetable 1

Mexican Chicken and Noodles

Another crowd-pleaser!

2 boneless, skinless chicken breasts (3 ounces each),
    cooked in 1 1/2 cups chicken broth over low heat for
    7 to 10 minutes and cooled
Nonfat nonstick cooking spray
1 green bell pepper, chopped
1 medium onion, chopped
1 3/4 cups fat-free chicken broth
1 teaspoon crushed garlic
1 can (10 ounces) Rotel diced tomatoes and green chilies
3 tablespoons flour
1 tablespoon Molly McButter dry butter flavor sprinkles*
8 slices (1 ounce each) fat-free American cheese, diced or
    cut into small pieces
1/4 teaspoon pepper
Salt, optional
1 package (7 ounces) No Yolk noodles or dumplings,
    cooked

Dice chicken breasts and set aside. Spray large skillet
with cooking spray and sauté green pepper and onion for
3 to 4 minutes over medium-low heat. Add 1/4 cup chicken
broth and garlic, and continue cooking about 5 minutes.
Add tomatoes and chilies.

*This can be found in small bottles in the baking supplies section of the market.

In small mixing bowl, whisk together flour, butter flavor sprinkles, and 1 ½ cups chicken broth until smooth. Pour into skillet and cook, stirring until mixture thickens. Add cheese, stirring until melted. Season with pepper and salt, if desired. Stir noodles and diced chicken into mixture and serve.

Recipe makes 4 servings.

Each serving provides:

405	Calories	2.8 g	Fat
36.8 g	Protein	0.48 g	Saturated fat
58.3 g	Carbohydrate	37 mg	Cholesterol

Diabetic exchanges: Lean meat, 2; vegetable, 1; starch, 2 ½

Orange Beef and Vegetable Stir Fry

———— ❦ ————

Wonderful blend of flavors! Serve over cooked rice.

1 pound round steak
$^{1}/_{4}$ cup soy sauce
$^{1}/_{4}$ cup rice vinegar
1 cup orange juice
6 packets Equal sweetener
1 tablespoon canola or olive oil
1 teaspoon minced garlic
1 teaspoon minced fresh ginger
1 red bell pepper, sliced
1 green bell pepper, sliced
2 carrots, thinly sliced
6 green onions, cut into 1-inch pieces (both green and
    white parts)
$^{1}/_{2}$ pound mushrooms, sliced
2 tablespoons cornstarch

Trim any extra fat from round steak. Slice into thin strips, against the grain. Mix soy sauce, vinegar, orange juice, and sweetener in small bowl. Pour over beef strips and place in refrigerator to marinate 6 to 8 hours.

When ready to cook, remove beef from marinade, reserving the liquid. Heat large skillet or wok to medium-high heat and add oil, swirling to coat bottom and sides of pan. Toss garlic and ginger into pan, stirring for 1 minute, then add drained beef. Stir and cook 3 to 4 minutes. Add red and green peppers, carrots, onions, and mushrooms to skillet, stirring to mix with beef. Cook and stir 4 to 5 minutes. Mix cornstarch into the marinade (a whisk is mighty handy for this) and pour cornstarch mixture into skillet, stirring into meat and vegetable mixture until thickened.

Recipe makes 6 servings.

Each serving provides:

194	Calories	5.7 g	Fat
20.7 g	Protein	1.31 g	Saturated fat
15.0 g	Carbohydrate	43 mg	Cholesterol

Diabetic exchanges: Lean meat, 3½; vegetable, 1

Paprika Chicken

———— ✌ ————

My, this is yummy! Serve over rice.

$1/3$ cup plus 2 tablespoons flour
1 tablespoon paprika
$1/2$ teaspoon salt
$1/8$ teaspoon pepper
Nonfat nonstick cooking spray
4 boneless, skinless chicken breasts (3 ounces each)
1 large onion, chopped
$2 1/2$ cups fat-free chicken broth
1 chicken bouillon cube, dissolved in $1/2$ cup hot water
$1/2$ cup light sour cream
2 tablespoons flour

In large bowl, mix $1/3$ cup flour, paprika, salt, and pepper. Spray large skillet well with cooking spray and heat over medium-high heat. Dredge chicken breasts in flour mixture, and brown on both sides in heated skillet. Cover chicken breasts with chopped onion. Pour 1 cup chicken broth and the bouillon over chicken and onions. Cover skillet and reduce heat to low. Simmer until chicken is done, 20 to 30 minutes.

Place cooked chicken on hot platter. Add remaining 1½ cups chicken broth and sour cream to drippings in skillet. Stir well over medium heat. Use a whisk or fork to stir in 2 tablespoons flour. Continue stirring until thickened. Pour over chicken.

Recipe makes 4 servings.

Each serving provides:

272	Calories	7.2 g	Fat
31.4 g	Protein	3.19 g	Saturated fat
19.1 g	Carbohydrate	85 mg	Cholesterol

Diabetic exchanges: Lean meat, 4; starch, ¾

Pasta Primavera

———— ❧ ————

This is an all-time favorite. Delightful flavor and beautiful colors make this a good choice if you are having company for dinner.

Pasta and Vegetables
1 cup chopped fresh broccoli pieces
1 cup sliced carrots
1 cup sliced zucchini
1 1/2 cups sliced fresh mushrooms
1 large tomato, chopped
1 cup fresh snow peas
4 cups cooked linguine noodles

Sauce
1/2 cup evaporated skim milk
1 cup skim milk
3/4 cup fat-free chicken broth
1/2 cup fat-free sour cream
1/2 cup fat-free Parmesan cheese
3 cloves garlic, pressed
2 tablespoons flour
Salt and black pepper

Steam or sauté vegetables 5 to 10 minutes while preparing sauce. Do not overcook. In medium saucepan, combine evaporated and regular skim milk, chicken broth, sour cream, Parmesan cheese, and garlic. In a small bowl, mix three tablespoons sauce with flour to make a thin paste. Add paste to sauce in pan and cook, stirring, over medium heat until sauce thickens. Place vegetables over noodles, pour sauce over top, and add salt and pepper to taste. Serve and enjoy.

Recipe makes 8 servings.

Each serving provides:

186	Calories	0.8 g	Fat
9.7 g	Protein	0.16 g	Saturated fat
34.7 g	Carbohydrate	4 mg	Cholesterol

Diabetic exchanges: Skim milk, ½; vegetable, 2; starch, 1

Italian Pasta and Vegetables

❧

This is delicious! We particularly like it prepared with angel hair pasta.

Nonfat nonstick cooking spray
1 medium onion, chopped
3 cloves garlic, minced
$1/4$ cup white cooking wine
$1/2$ cup fat-free chicken broth
1 tablespoon Molly McButter dry butter flavor sprinkles*
1 jar (8 ounces) roasted red peppers packed in water,
    drained and chopped
1 cup sliced raw zucchini
1 cup sliced raw mushrooms
3 cups cooked pasta
$1/3$ cup toasted pine nuts

*This can be found in small bottles in the baking supplies section of the market.

Spray large skillet with cooking spray and place over medium heat. Place onion and garlic in skillet, and cook, stirring for about 2 minutes. Add wine, chicken broth, and butter flavor sprinkles to skillet, stirring well to blend. Lower heat and simmer about 10 minutes. Add peppers, zucchini, and mushrooms, and stir. Serve hot over cooked pasta, topped with toasted pine nuts.

Recipe makes 3 servings.

Each serving provides:

365	Calories	10.6 g	Fat
14.0 g	Protein	1.57 g	Saturated fat
56.1 g	Carbohydrate	0 mg	Cholesterol

Diabetic exchanges: Starch, 3; vegetable, 4½

Pepperoni Pizza Rolls

—❦—

These are so good, you'll think you are eating something sinful!

Nonfat nonstick butter-flavored cooking spray
1 roll (7½ ounces) refrigerated biscuits*
¾ cup Ragu pizza sauce
20 slices of Hormel turkey pepperoni, chopped in small
     pieces
1 cup shredded Kraft fat-free mozzarella cheese
Garlic powder
Onion powder

Preheat oven to 425 degrees F

Spray large baking sheet with cooking spray. Remove one biscuit from roll and place on clean dry surface. Using a rolling pin, roll biscuit out to about the size of the palm of your hand. Spread 1 tablespoon pizza sauce in center of dough, add about 2 teaspoons chopped pepperoni and 1 tablespoon shredded cheese. Sprinkle on a little garlic powder and onion powder. Bring sides of dough to the center and pinch tops together or roll each like a pencil. Place on baking sheet.

*The cheapest brands usually contain the least fat, 1½ grams for 2 biscuits.

Repeat process for all remaining biscuits. After all rolls are placed on baking sheet, spray tops lightly with cooking spray. Bake at 425 degrees F for 10 to 13 minutes.

Recipe makes 10 rolls. One serving equals 2 rolls.

Each serving provides:

172	Calories	3.3 g	Fat
12.3 g	Protein	0.83 g	Saturated fat
24.0 g	Carbohydrate	8 mg	Cholesterol

Diabetic exchanges: Lean meat, 1; vegetable, 1; starch, 1

Pepper Steak

———— ✤ ————

This is our version of an "oldie but goodie." Serve over rice.

1 pound sirloin or round steak
Nonfat nonstick cooking spray
1 green bell pepper, sliced
1 red bell pepper, sliced
1 medium onion, sliced
2 tablespoons soy sauce
$^1/_2$ cup cooking wine (any kind)
1 teaspoon minced garlic
1 can (10$^1/_2$ ounces) beef broth
2 tablespoons cornstarch
$^1/_4$ cup water

Slice steak into thin strips, across grain. Spray large skillet with cooking spray and place over medium-high heat. Sauté green and red pepper and onion slices, stirring often, for 3 to 4 minutes. Remove from skillet and set aside. Quickly brown steak strips in hot skillet, stirring and turning as they cook. Lower heat and add soy sauce, cooking wine, and garlic to skillet. Simmer 10 minutes, then add beef broth and return vegetables to skillet. Simmer 5 minutes. Mix cornstarch and water together, then add to skillet, stirring to thicken.

Recipe makes 6 servings.

Each serving provides:

168	Calories	3.2 g	Fat
19.6 g	Protein	1.12 g	Saturated fat
9.3 g	Carbohydrate	44 mg	Cholesterol

Diabetic exchanges: Lean protein, 2; vegetable, 2

Pizza Rolls

—✤—

A fun meal that is great to tuck into lunch boxes the next day. These can also be cut into bite-sized pieces and served at a party.

Nonfat nonstick cooking spray
6 egg roll wrappers*
$^1/_2$ cup lowfat pizza sauce
12 slices Hormel turkey pepperoni, chopped into small
    pieces
1$^1/_2$ cups grated fat-free mozzarella cheese
1 egg white, slightly beaten

Preheat oven to 375 degrees F

Spray large baking sheet with cooking spray. Place one eggroll wrapper on a large plate and spread about 1$^1/_2$ tablespoons pizza sauce over the center of the surface, leaving about one-half inch around the edge. Sprinkle about 2 teaspoons of pepperoni pieces on top of sauce, then sprinkle about $^1/_4$ cup cheese over surface. Start at one corner

*These are usually found in the produce section of the market.

and roll. About halfway during the rolling, fold the two sides in and continue rolling.

Place finished roll on baking sheet and brush with egg white. Repeat same procedure for all remaining rolls. Place in oven and bake at 375 degrees F for 15 to 18 minutes. Serve and enjoy.

Recipe makes 6 rolls. One serving equals 2 rolls.

Each serving provides:

274	Calories	1.6 g	Fat
27.3 g	Protein	0.34 g	Saturated fat
39.7 g	Carbohydrate	14 mg	Cholesterol

Diabetic exchanges: Starch, 2; vegetable, 1; lean protein, 1 ½

Pepperoni Mini Pizzas

———— ❦ ————

What an easy treat for the cook! These pizzas will appeal
to kids of all ages . . . even those who remember when "I
Like Ike" was a campaign slogan.

Nonfat nonstick cooking spray
1 package (8 ounces) small Boboli pizza crusts, 2 per
    package
$\frac{1}{2}$ cup Ragu pizza sauce
20 slices Hormel turkey pepperoni, chopped in small
    pieces
1 cup shredded Kraft fat-free mozzarella cheese
Garlic powder
Onion powder

Preheat oven to 425 degrees F

Spray medium baking sheet with cooking spray. Spread
both crust tops with about $\frac{1}{4}$ cup pizza sauce each.
Sprinkle with pepperoni pieces. Add cheese and a sprinkling of garlic and onion powders. Place pizzas on baking
sheet. Bake at 425 degrees F for 10 to 13 minutes. Remove from oven and serve hot.

Recipe makes 4 servings. One serving equals $\frac{1}{2}$ pizza.

Each serving provides:

221	Calories	5.0 g	Fat
18.1 g	Protein	0.85 g	Saturated fat
28.1 g	Carbohydrate	13 mg	Cholesterol

Diabetic exchanges: Lean protein, 1; vegetable, 1; starch, 2

Our Favorite Pizza Crust

—❦—

This also makes *great* breadsticks.

2 cups flour
1 teaspoon salt
1 teaspoon sugar
³/₄ cup warm water
2 teaspoons dry yeast
1 teaspoon olive oil

Combine flour, salt, and sugar in a large mixing bowl. In a smaller bowl, combine water and yeast, stirring until yeast is dissolved. Combine two mixtures in large bowl and add oil, stirring until dough forms into ball. Turn dough out onto a lightly floured surface and knead until smooth and elastic, about 5 minutes. Place dough in a 2-quart plastic or glass container that has a tight-fitting lid or use plastic wrap to tightly cover bowl. Place bowl in a warm place (about 85 degrees F) and let dough rise until doubled, at least 1 hour. When ready to bake pizza, preheat oven to 450 degrees F. Lightly oil a large pizza pan. Punch dough down, and pat evenly into pizza pan. Bake crust at 450 degrees F for 5 minutes.

Recipe makes 8 servings.

Each serving provides:

122	Calories	0.9 g	Fat
3.4 g	Protein	0.12 g	Saturated fat
24.5 g	Carbohydrate	0 mg	Cholesterol

Diabetic exchange: Starch, 1 ¹/₂

Pork Tenders in Gravy

—✦—

For when you want to fix something extra special. The flour used to coat the pork gives this dish its wonderful gravy. Serve this over rice for a company dinner. Great comfort food!

2 pounds pork tenderloin, cut into $1/2$- to 1-inch cubes
$1/3$ cup flour
Nonfat nonstick cooking spray
1 medium onion, chopped
1 green bell pepper, chopped
3 cups water
1 cup white cooking wine
$1/4$ cup soy sauce
$1/4$ cup Worcestershire sauce
1 teaspoon garlic powder
1 teaspoon seasoned salt
Salt and pepper

Coat pork cubes with flour. Spray dutch oven well with cooking spray and place over medium heat. Sauté onion and green pepper 5 to 10 minutes or until tender. Remove and set aside. Again spray bottom of pan and place over medium-high heat. Add pork cubes, stirring to brown. Return onions and green pepper to pot and add water, wine, soy sauce, Worcestershire sauce, garlic powder, and seasoned salt. Add salt and pepper to taste. Cover dutch oven and simmer over low heat for 30 minutes. Uncover and simmer about 15 minutes longer.

Note: If you wish to make the gravy thicker, mix together 2 table-spoons flour and ¹/₂ cup hot water or broth and stir into the pork mixture as it is bubbling.

Recipe makes 8 servings.

Each serving provides:

202	Calories	4.2 g	Fat
25.9 g	Protein	1.43 g	Saturated fat
8.9 g	Carbohydrate	79 mg	Cholesterol

Diabetic exchanges: Lean protein, 3; vegetable, 2

Spicy Noodles

―――― ❧ ――――

We absolutely love the exotic blend of flavors in this dish.
One of our favorites!

2 medium carrots, thinly sliced
1 package frozen Reames Free fat-free noodles
$1/2$ cup reduced-fat peanut butter
1 tablespoon dark sesame oil*
2 tablespoons soy sauce
2 tablespoons rice vinegar
3 packets Equal sweetener
$1/4$ teaspoon red pepper flakes
4 green onions, chopped
$1/4$ cup chopped fresh cilantro
$1/4$ cup chopped peanuts

Steam carrot slices until almost tender. Cook noodles
according to package directions. In blender or food processor, mix peanut butter, sesame oil, soy sauce, vinegar,
sweetener, and pepper flakes. Blend until smooth. In a
large serving bowl, combine hot, drained noodles, peanut
butter mixture, carrots, green onions, cilantro, and peanuts.

Recipe makes 4 servings.

Each serving provides:

516	Calories	19.0 g	Fat
19.7 g	Protein	3.47 g	Saturated fat
66.8 g	Carbohydrate	0 mg	Cholesterol

Diabetic exchanges: Starch, 3; vegetable, 2;
medium fat protein, 1; fat, 3

---

*This can be found in the Oriental foods section of the market.

Rice Pilaf

This is especially tasty when served with chicken.

Nonfat nonstick cooking spray
1 large onion, chopped
1/4 cup canned mushrooms
1/4 cup chopped green bell pepper
1 cup uncooked white rice
1/2 cup liquid Butter Buds (prepared using 1 packet mixed
    with 1/2 cup hot water)
1/8 teaspoon thyme
2 cups fat-free chicken broth

Preheat oven to 350 degrees F

Spray large skillet with cooking spray and sauté onion over
medium heat for about 5 minutes. Add mushrooms and
green pepper and continue cooking 5 to 10 minutes. Remove vegetables, reduce heat, and pour rice into skillet.
Stir rice over low heat, browning slightly. Add Butter Buds.
Return vegetables and add thyme. In small pan, heat
chicken broth to boiling and stir into rice mixture. Pour all
into large casserole dish. Cover and bake at 350 degrees F
until liquid is absorbed and rice is tender, 30 to 40 minutes.

Recipe makes 4 servings.

Each serving provides:

214	Calories	0.6 g	Fat
5.3 g	Protein	0.19 g	Saturated fat
46.1 g	Carbohydrate	0 mg	Cholesterol

Diabetic exchanges: Starch, 2; vegetable, 2

Hearty Ranch Biscuit Bake

——— ✥ ———

This is one of our very tastiest dishes!

Biscuit Topping
2 1/2 cups reduced-fat Bisquick biscuit mix
1 cup skim milk
1/2 cup grated fat-free cheese

Stew
Nonfat nonstick cooking spray
1 medium onion, chopped
1 pound ground turkey breast
2 stalks celery, chopped
1/4 cup ketchup
1/4 cup water
1 tablespoon lemon juice
1 1/2 teaspoons brown sugar substitute
1 teaspoon Worcestershire sauce
1 teaspoon salt
1 teaspoon vinegar
1/4 teaspoon dry mustard
1 can (16 ounces) Mexican or ranch-style beans
2 tablespoons chili powder

In medium bowl, thoroughly blend biscuit mix, skim milk, and cheese. On clean, dry surface, lightly dusted with flour or biscuit mix, roll out dough with roller and cut with biscuit cutter. (Makes about 6 biscuits)

Preheat oven to 400 degrees F

Spray large skillet with cooking spray. Brown onion and turkey breast and then add celery, ketchup, water, lemon juice, brown sugar substitute, Worcestershire sauce, salt, vinegar, dry mustard, beans, and chili powder. Cover and simmer over low heat for 15 minutes. Pour into large casserole dish and top with biscuits. Bake at 400 degrees F until biscuits are golden brown, 15 to 25 minutes.

Recipe makes 6 servings.

Each serving provides:

429	Calories	6.7 g	Fat
31.1 g	Protein	1.61 g	Saturated fat
59.5 g	Carbohydrate	50 mg	Cholesterol

Diabetic exchanges: Lean meat, 3; starch, 3; vegetable, 1

Hearty Skillet Breakfast

———— ✦ ————

You don't have to save this for breakfast. . . . This is great anytime! Serve topped with salsa, if desired. Avocados are great with this, too.

Nonfat nonstick cooking spray
$1/2$ red bell pepper, thinly sliced
$1/2$ green bell pepper, thinly sliced
1 medium onion, sliced
2 cloves garlic, minced
3 to 4 tablespoons cooking wine (any kind)
$1/4$ teaspoon Italian seasoning
2 medium potatoes, baked and cubed
1 cup fat-free liquid egg product
1 tablespoon Molly McButter dry butter flavor sprinkles*
Salt and pepper
1 cup grated fat-free mozzarella cheese

Spray large skillet with cooking spray and place over medium heat. Sauté red and green peppers and onion for 5 minutes. Add garlic, cooking wine, and Italian seasoning, and continue to cook for 5 more minutes. Add potatoes, allowing them to brown slightly on all sides. In a

*This can be found in small bottles in the baking supplies section of the market.

small bowl, mix egg product, butter flavor sprinkles, and salt and pepper as desired, and pour over potatoes in skillet. Stir and cook until eggs are set. Sprinkle mozzarella over top of mixture. Place lid on skillet and remove from heat, allowing cheese to melt.

Recipe makes 4 servings.

Each serving provides:

175	Calories	0.2 g	Fat
16.3 g	Protein	0.04 g	Saturated fat
24.9 g	Carbohydrate	5 mg	Cholesterol

Diabetic exchanges: Lean meat, 1; starch, 1; vegetable, 1

Chicken Sour Cream Enchiladas

Bound to become a family favorite.

Nonfat nonstick cooking spray
8 (6-inch) flour tortillas
2½ cups hot chicken broth
2 cups chopped chicken breast
1 medium onion, chopped
2 cups grated light Cheddar cheese
2 tablespoons flour
1 tablespoon Molly McButter dry butter flavor sprinkles*
1 cup light sour cream
1 can (4½ ounces) chopped green chilies

Preheat oven to 350 degrees F

Spray large (10 × 15-inch) baking dish with cooking spray.
Dip each tortilla into the hot broth to soften. One at a
time, lay softened tortillas in baking dish and fill with
chicken, onion, and cheese. Roll and place seam-side
down.

*This can be found in small bottles in the baking supplies section of the market.

In saucepan, mix the broth, flour, and butter flavor sprinkles with whisk. Stir over medium heat until slightly thickened. Add sour cream and chilies, and pour over enchiladas. Bake at 350 degrees F for 20 minutes.

Recipe makes 8 servings. One serving equals 1 enchilada.

Each serving provides:

273	Calories	10.5 g	Fat
22.6 g	Protein	6.01 g	Saturated fat
21.0 g	Carbohydrate	62 mg	Cholesterol

Diabetic exchanges: Starch, 2; lowfat protein, 2

Old-Fashioned Beef Stew

The next time cold weather calls for stew, try this scrumpti/ous version.

2 pounds beef round rump roast, cut into 1-inch cubes
1/2 cup flour
1 tablespoon oil
3 cups water
1 cup cooking wine (any kind)
1 tablespoon beef bouillon granules (or 2 beef bouillon cubes)
5 medium potatoes, peeled and cubed
4 carrots, scraped and cut into chunks
2 medium onions, chopped
Salt and pepper

Coat beef cubes with flour. Heat large Dutch oven over medium-high heat, pour oil over bottom of pan, and brown beef cubes on all sides. Add water, wine, and bouillon. Cover and simmer over low heat 1 1/2 to 2 hours. Add potatoes, carrots, and onions. Cover and simmer 1 hour more. Add salt and pepper to taste.

Note: Add canned diced tomatoes or chopped fresh tomatoes with other vegetables, if desired.

Recipe makes about 8 servings.

Each serving provides:

343	Calories	9.3 g	Fat
28.1 g	Protein	2.76 g	Saturated fat
30.4 g	Carbohydrate	68 mg	Cholesterol

Diabetic exchanges: Medium protein, 3; starch, 1; vegetable, 2

Sweet Spicy Chicken Breasts

Adjust the "heat" in this dish to your own tolerance level. We like it pretty hot. Also great served over rice.

Nonfat nonstick cooking spray
4 boneless, skinless chicken breasts (4 ounces each)
1 can (14½ ounces) fat-free chicken broth
2 tablespoons dry onion flakes
⅓ cup green jalapeño Tabasco sauce
1 tablespoon sugar
1 clove garlic, pressed
1½ tablespoons cornstarch
1 medium Anaheim pepper, seeded and sliced
1 jalapeño pepper, seeded and sliced, optional*
2 cups coarsely grated carrot
½ green bell pepper, sliced
3 tablespoons Equal sweetener

Spray large skillet with cooking spray. Brown chicken breasts on both sides. Remove chicken and add chicken broth, onion flakes, Tabasco, sugar, garlic, cornstarch, Anaheim pepper, and jalapeño pepper, if desired. Stir constantly over medium heat until sauce starts to thicken.

*Depending on how hot you like it, omit for milder taste.

Return chicken to skillet; cover and simmer over very low heat for 8 to 10 minutes, stirring occasionally. Add carrots and green pepper. Cover and simmer for 3 to 5 minutes until vegetables reach desired tenderness. Stir in Equal just before serving.

Recipe makes 4 servings.

Each serving provides:

258	Calories	3.3 g	Fat
38.3 g	Protein	0.90 g	Saturated fat
18.5 g	Carbohydrate	73 mg	Cholesterol

Diabetic exchanges: Lean meat, 4; vegetable, 1

Taco Rolls

---❦---

Spicy little bundles . . . bound to excite!

Nonfat nonstick cooking spray
$1/2$ pound ground turkey breast
1 jar (8 ounces) taco sauce
1 tablespoon dry onion flakes
$1 1/2$ tablespoons dry taco seasoning
6 eggroll wrappers*
6 tablespoons grated fat-free Cheddar cheese
1 egg white, slightly beaten

Preheat oven to 375 degrees F

Spray medium skillet with cooking spray and brown
ground turkey. Add taco sauce, onion flakes, and taco
seasoning. Stir and simmer over low heat for about 5
minutes, until meat is thoroughly cooked.

Spray large baking sheet with cooking spray. Place
one eggroll wrapper on large plate and cover the center
with meat mixture, leaving about $1/2$ inch around the edge.
Sprinkle about 1 tablespoon grated cheese over meat.

*These are usually found in the produce section of the market.

Start at one corner and roll. About halfway through the rolling, fold each side in and continue rolling. Place finished roll on baking sheet and brush with egg white. Repeat procedure with remaining rolls. Bake at 375 degrees F for 15 to 18 minutes. Serve hot.

Recipe makes 6 rolls. One serving equals 2 rolls.

Each serving provides:

161	Calories	0.7 g	Fat
15.8 g	Protein	0.41 g	Saturated fat
23.1 g	Carbohydrate	24 mg	Cholesterol

Diabetic exchanges: Starch, 1; lean meat, 2

Homestyle Skillet Stew

—✤—

Such a delicious, satisfying meal, *and* it's so easy!

1 medium potato, peeled and cut into small chunks
3 medium carrots, peeled and cut into small chunks
1 small onion, cut into quarters
Nonfat nonstick cooking spray
1 pound ground turkey breast
1/3 cup fat-free sour cream
1 cup skim milk
1 package (1 ounce) ranch dressing mix

Cook potato, carrots, and onion in small amount of water in microwave until tender. Set aside. Spray large skillet with cooking spray. Brown ground turkey breast. Add sour cream, milk, and ranch dressing mix. Stir and simmer 1 to 2 minutes. Add cooked vegetables and stir and simmer 1 to 2 minutes more.

Recipe makes 6 servings.

Each serving provides:

162	Calories	1.4 g	Fat
22.5 g	Protein	0.45 g	Saturated fat
14.1 g	Carbohydrate	46 mg	Cholesterol

Diabetic exchanges: Lean meat, 2; vegetable, 2

Tender Smothered Pork and Potatoes

This is the best, most amazingly delicious dinner ever!!!

1 pound pork tenderloin
Flour
Nonfat nonstick cooking spray
1 can (10³/₄ ounces) Campbell's Healthy Request cream of
    mushroom soup
1¹/₄ cups skim milk
2 large potatoes, sliced
Salt and black pepper, optional

Use a sharp knife to cut the pork tenderloin into thin
(¹/₄- to ¹/₂-inch thick) slices. Dust pork slices with flour.
Spray large skillet with cooking spray and place over
medium heat. Place pork slices in skillet, turning to brown
on both sides. Reduce heat to low. In a small bowl, combine mushroom soup and milk, mixing well, and pour
over pork slices. Arrange potato slices over smothered
pork, spooning some of the mushroom soup mixture over
potatoes. Add salt and pepper, as desired. Tightly cover
skillet and simmer until potatoes are done, 30 to 45 minutes.

Recipe makes 6 servings.

Each serving provides:

224	Calories	6.6 g	Fat
20.9 g	Protein	2.00 g	Saturated fat
19.1 g	Carbohydrate	52 mg	Cholesterol

Diabetic exchanges: Starch, 1; lean protein, 2¹/₂

Vegetarian Enchiladas

———— ❧ ————

Scrumptious and festive, these enchiladas will rival those in any restaurant! Garnish with salsa or fat-free sour cream, if desired.

Enchiladas
Nonfat nonstick cooking spray
1 carrot, sliced
1/2 cup fat-free chicken broth
1 1/2 cups fresh sliced mushrooms
1 small zucchini, sliced
1 small yellow squash, sliced
1 medium onion, sliced
2 fresh green chilies, sliced
1 tablespoon fresh cilantro, chopped
1 package (1 1/4 ounces) dry taco seasoning
1/2 teaspoon garlic powder
1 clove garlic, pressed
1 medium tomato, chopped
Salt and black pepper
6 small fat-free flour tortillas

Sauce
1/2 cup evaporated skim milk
1/2 cup shredded fat-free mozzarella cheese
2 green onions, chopped
1/4 teaspoon garlic powder

Preheat oven to 350 degrees F

Spray large skillet with cooking spray. Add carrot and
1/4 cup of chicken broth. Simmer and stir 2 to 3 minutes.
Add mushrooms and simmer another 2 to 3 minutes. Add
zucchini, yellow squash, onion, green chilies, cilantro, taco
seasoning, garlic powder, and pressed garlic. Pour in re-
mainder of chicken broth and simmer until vegetables
are partially done. Add tomato and cook about 1 minute.
Do not overcook; leave some crunch in the vegetables.
Remove from heat and cool slightly. Add salt and pepper
to taste.

Spray large baking dish with cooking spray. Place
about 1/2 cup vegetable mixture on each flour tortilla and
roll. Place rolls in baking dish.

In small bowl, combine milk, cheese, green onions,
and garlic powder. Pour over enchiladas and bake at 350
degrees F for 25 to 30 minutes.

Recipe makes 6 servings.

Each serving provides:

155	Calories	0.8 g	Fat
9.0 g	Protein	0.25 g	Saturated fat
28.9 g	Carbohydrate	2 mg	Cholesterol

Diabetic exchanges: Starch, 1; vegetable, 3

Grilled Italian Veggie Sandwich

This is otherwise known as Doris's Deluxe Sandwich . . . and we *love* it!

Nonfat nonstick cooking spray
1 small to medium zucchini, sliced flat lengthwise
Garlic powder or salt
Black pepper
Italian seasoning
1 small to medium yellow crookneck squash, sliced flat lengthwise
1 medium onion, sliced
1 red bell pepper, cut into quarters
2 hoagie buns, sliced
2 slices Kraft fat-free mozzarella cheese
1 medium tomato, sliced
1 marinated artichoke heart
2 tablespoons Parmesan cheese

Preheat oven to 425 degrees F

Spray large skillet with cooking spray. Place slices of zucchini in skillet over medium heat and brown on both sides. While browning, sprinkle with garlic powder or salt, black pepper, and Italian seasoning. When browned, remove to a plate. Repeat this procedure for yellow squash, onion, and bell pepper. Cooking time depends on personal taste. I like a little texture left in the vegetables for this sandwich, but if you prefer your vegetables cooked longer, that is fine.

Spray large baking pan or sheet with cooking spray. Place the bottoms of the two hoagie buns on pan. Cut one slice of cheese in half and place lengthwise on bun. Repeat for second bun. Layer the grilled vegetables and sliced tomato on each sandwich in any order you choose. Use ½ artichoke and 1 tablespoon Parmesan cheese per sandwich. Place tops on each bun and bake at 425 degrees F for 5 minutes. Cut in half and serve warm.

Recipe makes 4 servings. One serving equals ½ sandwich.

Each serving provides:

285	Calories	4.8 g	Fat
13.4 g	Protein	1.15 g	Saturated fat
46.9 g	Carbohydrate	5 mg	Cholesterol

Diabetic exchanges: Lean protein, 1; starch, 2; vegetable, 3

Potluck Casserole

❧

You *must* try this casserole! You won't believe how good it is. Okay, the ingredients sound a bit strange, but even if you have invited culinary snobs to dinner they will rave about this dish.

Nonfat nonstick cooking spray
1 medium onion, chopped
1 green pepper, chopped
1 pound ground turkey breast
1 teaspoon garlic salt
1 can (10³/₄ ounces) Campbell's Healthy Request cream of
    mushroom soup
1 can Franco American spaghetti
¹/₂ cup fat-free Cheddar cheese
Salt and pepper

Preheat oven to 400 degrees F

Spray a large skillet with cooking spray and sauté the onion, green pepper, and turkey breast over medium heat. Stir in garlic salt, mushroom soup, spaghetti, and cheese. Add salt and pepper to taste.

Spray large casserole dish with cooking spray. Pour mixture into casserole dish and bake at 400 degrees F for 10 to 15 minutes.

Recipe makes 4 servings.

Each serving provides:

297	Calories	3.9 g	Fat
34.9 g	Protein	1.06 g	Saturated fat
28.5 g	Carbohydrate	75 mg	Cholesterol

Diabetic exchanges: Lean protein, 4; vegetable, 3

Grilled Vegetables with Chicken

This meal is one of those that makes you think life is perfect. It's delicious *and* so pretty you will wish you had invited company, just so they could be impressed.

2 medium carrots
1 medium red potato
1 medium onion, quartered
1 small zucchini squash
1 small yellow crookneck squash
1 red bell pepper
Approximately ½ bottle (12.7 ounces) Allegro marinade,
    hickory smoke flavor
2 boneless, skinless chicken breasts (3 ounces each)

Precook whole carrots, potato, and onion in microwave until slightly tender. ***Do not cook until done***. Because of differences in microwave ovens and sizes of vegetables, it is difficult to say exactly how long to cook these. Try 3 minutes to start, and cook to desired doneness from there. After microwaving, cut potato and onion in half. Do not slice carrots. Cut squash and bell pepper in half. Place all vegetables in large, resealable plastic storage bag. Pour about ¾ cup marinade into bag and let vegetables marinate for several hours. Turn vegetables every 30 minutes. Place chicken in separate zip-lock bag and add about ½ cup marinade (add more if necessary). Place bag of chicken in refrigerator and marinate for several hours, also turning every 30 minutes.*

Prepare grill for cooking. When fire is ready, place vegetables and chicken on grill. Cook on all sides to desired doneness.

Recipe makes 2 servings.

Each serving provides:

261	Calories	3.6 g	Fat
30.3 g	Protein	0.96 g	Saturated fat
27.7 g	Carbohydrate	72 mg	Cholesterol

Diabetic exchanges: Lean protein, 4; vegetable, 2

---

*After chicken is marinated, discard marinade and *do not* re-use.

Layered Potato Bake

—❧—

If you enjoy baked potatoes with different toppings, you're bound to love this. You may want to substitute your own favorites for the ones we use here, or simply add to these. Yum!

4 medium potatoes, baked
1 cup light sour cream
2 tablespoons Molly McButter dry butter flavor sprinkles*
Pepper
Nonfat nonstick butter-flavored cooking spray
1 medium onion, chopped
1 green bell pepper, chopped
1 cup lowfat ham, finely chopped
1 cup light cheese, grated

Preheat oven to 350 degrees F

While potatoes are still hot from baking, scoop flesh out of skins and mash with sour cream and butter flavor sprinkles. Add pepper to taste. Spray a 9-inch pie plate with cooking spray and add mashed potatoes, spreading mixture to fill dish. Spray a medium skillet with cooking

*This can be found in small bottles in the baking supplies section of the market.

spray and sauté onion and green pepper. (A small amount of cooking wine or chicken broth is useful to keep veggies moist as they sauté.) Spoon cooked onions and green peppers onto potatoes. Top with ham and cheese. Bake at 350 degrees F until dish is heated through and cheese is melted. Cut into wedges to serve.

Recipe makes 6 servings.

Each serving provides:

259	Calories	8.1 g	Fat
15.3 g	Protein	4.66 g	Saturated fat
29.8 g	Carbohydrate	39 mg	Cholesterol

Diabetic exchanges: Medium meat, 2; starch, 1; vegetable, 1

Asian Peanut Chicken on Rice

If you like spicy-hot Szechwan Chinese dishes, try this variation of a favorite, Kung Pao Chicken. This makes everyone rave! Serve over rice.

Sauce
3 tablespoons soy sauce
2 tablespoons rice vinegar
2 tablespoons cooking sherry
$^{1}/_{3}$ cup chicken broth
2 packets Equal sweetener
1 tablespoon cornstarch

Chicken
2 boneless, skinless chicken breasts (4 ounces each),
    cooked
1 tablespoon peanut oil
1 teaspoon minced garlic
1 teaspoon minced fresh ginger
4 green onions, cut into 1-inch pieces (both white and
    green parts)
$^{1}/_{2}$ cup chopped dry-roasted peanuts
$^{1}/_{4}$ teaspoon crushed red pepper flakes

In small bowl, mix soy sauce, vinegar, sherry, chicken broth, sweetener, and cornstarch. Set aside. Cut chicken into small pieces (½-inch). Heat wok or large skillet over medium-high heat. Pour 1 tablespoon peanut oil into skillet then add garlic and ginger. Stir quickly for only about 15 seconds, then add green onions, peanuts, and crushed red pepper. Stir and cook only about 30 seconds, then add sauce and chicken pieces. Stir until sauce is thickened.

Recipe makes 3 servings.

Each serving provides:

308	Calories	16.5 g	Fat
30.0 g	Protein	2.83 g	Saturated fat
9.5 g	Carbohydrate	64 mg	Cholesterol

Diabetic exchanges: Lean protein, 4; vegetable, 1; fat, 1½

Breakfast Sausage Gravy and Biscuits

Invite the neighbors over for an old-fashioned breakfast.

Biscuits
Use refrigerated canned biscuits that are either fat-free or 1 gram of fat per biscuit. You can also make your own using Pioneer Low-Fat Biscuit Mix or a light biscuit mix of your choice. I prefer Pioneer Low-Fat Biscuit Mix because of the excellent quality and flavor. Prepare according to package directions.

Gravy
Nonfat nonstick cooking spray
1 ounce ground turkey sausage, crumbled
4 tablespoons flour
1 cup fat-free chicken broth
1/2 cup evaporated skim milk
1 cup skim milk
2 teaspoons Molly McButter dry butter flavor sprinkles*
Salt and black pepper to taste

*This can be found in small bottles in the baking supplies section of the market.

In large skillet sprayed with nonstick cooking spray, brown crumbled turkey sausage. Add flour and lightly brown. In medium bowl, combine remaining ingredients. Stir with whisk and add to sausage mixture; stir until gravy thickens. Serve over hot biscuits.

Recipe makes 6 servings.

Each serving provides:

120	Calories	1.5 g	Fat
6.1 g	Protein	0.44 g	Saturated fat
20.0 g	Carbohydrate	5 mg	Cholesterol

Diabetic exchanges: Starch, 1; lean meat, $^1/_8$; skim milk, $^1/_3$

Tomato and Basil Pasta

———— ❧ ————

This is such a quick, delicious pasta sauce. The fresh basil is what really gives it a special flavor.

1 tablespoon olive oil
3 cloves garlic, minced
2 1/2 cups fresh peeled and cubed tomatoes
3/4 cup dry white wine
1/4 cup chopped fresh basil
1 teaspoon oregano
1/8 teaspoon red pepper flakes
Salt, optional

Heat olive oil in skillet over medium heat. Add garlic and cook only about a minute. Add tomatoes and cook another minute. Stir in wine, basil, oregano, and pepper flakes, and simmer for 10 minutes. Add salt, if desired. Serve over hot pasta.

Recipe makes 3 servings.

Each serving provides:

94	Calories	5.0 g	Fat
1.6 g	Protein	0.68 g	Saturated fat
8.6 g	Carbohydrate	0 mg	Cholesterol

Diabetic exchanges: Fat, 1/2; vegetable, 3

Buttermilk Chicken

Rich, old-fashioned flavor.

$^3/_4$ cup lowfat buttermilk
$^1/_4$ teaspoon garlic salt
2 cloves fresh garlic, pressed
Black pepper to taste
4 boneless, skinless chicken breasts (3 ounces each)
2 cups cornflakes, crushed
Nonfat nonstick cooking spray

Preheat oven to 350 degrees F

Mix together buttermilk, garlic salt, garlic, and black pepper. Dip chicken breasts in mixture, and then roll in crushed cornflakes.

Place on baking sheet sprayed with nonstick cooking spray and bake for 25 to 30 minutes.

Recipe makes 4 servings.

Each serving provides:

165	Calories	1.5 g	Fat
22.2 g	Protein	0.56 g	Saturated fat
14.9 g	Carbohydrate	51 mg	Cholesterol

Diabetic exchanges: Starch, $^2/_3$; lean meat, $1^2/_3$; skim milk, $^1/_4$

Cheese Bake with Spinach

———— ❧ ————

Wonderful as a dip or spread for a party.

$^1/_2$ cup frozen chopped spinach, thawed and drained
$1^3/_4$ cups 1-percent cottage cheese, drained
$^1/_2$ cup fat-free sour cream
$^1/_3$ cup fat-free liquid egg product
2 teaspoons dry onion flakes
2 tablespoons flour
Salt and black pepper to taste
$^1/_4$ cup plus 2 tablespoons Parmesan cheese
Nonfat nonstick cooking spray

Preheat oven to 325 degrees F

In large bowl, combine all ingredients, except 2 table-spoons Parmesan cheese and cooking spray, and stir with spoon. Pour into 8- or 9-inch square baking dish sprayed with nonstick cooking spray and sprinkle remaining Parmesan cheese over top. Bake for 30 to 40 minutes.

Recipe makes 6 servings.

Each serving provides:

108	Calories	2.3 g	Fat
13.7 g	Protein	1.43 g	Saturated fat
7.5 g	Carbohydrate	7 mg	Cholesterol

Diabetic exchanges: Starch, $^1/_8$; lean meat, $1^2/_3$; vegetable, $^1/_4$

Honey Dijon Baked Crispy Chicken

This dish has a wonderful mix of flavors.

³/₄ cup Kraft fat-free mayonnaise
1 tablespoon dry fat-free or lowfat Honey Dijon salad
    dressing mix
4 boneless, skinless chicken breasts (3 ounces each)
³/₄ cup crushed cornflakes
Nonfat nonstick cooking spray
Salt and black pepper to taste

Preheat oven to 350 degrees F

Mix together mayonnaise and dry salad dressing mix.
Pat dry the chicken breasts. Dip chicken in mayonnaise
mixture and roll in crushed cornflakes.

    Place on baking sheet or pan sprayed with nonstick
cooking spray. Season with salt and pepper. Bake for
30 to 35 minutes.

Recipe makes 4 servings.

Each serving provides:

186	Calories	1.3 g	Fat
20.7 g	Protein	0.36 g	Saturated fat
20.3 g	Carbohydrate	49 mg	Cholesterol

Diabetic exchanges: Starch, 1¹/₈; lean meat, 1²/₃

Chicken Breasts with Lemon Sauce

One of Doris's favorites—delicious!

4 boneless, skinless chicken breasts (3 ounces each)
Garlic salt to taste
Black pepper to taste
Nonfat nonstick cooking spray
1 cup fat-free chicken broth
1 1/2 tablespoons fresh lemon juice
1/2 teaspoon grated lemon peel
1/4 cup fat-free Parmesan cheese
1/3 cup fat-free sour cream
1 tablespoon all-purpose flour

Season chicken breasts with garlic salt and black pepper. Spray skillet with nonstick cooking spray. Add chicken breasts and brown and cook over medium heat until done, about 4 to 5 minutes on each side.

In medium saucepan, combine chicken broth, lemon juice, lemon peel, Parmesan cheese, and sour cream. Use whisk to stir until smooth. Add 2 to 3 tablespoons mixture to flour to make a thin paste. Stir paste back into sauce and stir over medium heat until thickened. Pour over cooked chicken breasts and serve.

Recipe makes 4 servings.

Each serving provides:

139	Calories	1.1 g	Fat
22.7 g	Protein	0.28 g	Saturated fat
7.3 g	Carbohydrate	52 mg	Cholesterol

Diabetic exchanges: Starch, $1/8$; lean meat, $2^1/3$

Chicken Breasts with Pimiento Sauce

Wonderful flavor.

2 boneless, skinless chicken breasts (4 ounces each)
1/4 teaspoon garlic powder
Black pepper to taste
1/2 cup fat-free cream cheese
2 tablespoons chopped pimiento
1 teaspoon dry onion flakes
1/4 cup fat-free chicken broth
1/4 cup fresh bell pepper, chopped
Nonfat nonstick cooking spray

Preheat oven to 350 degrees F

Season chicken breasts with garlic powder and pepper.

In medium bowl, combine cream cheese, pimiento, onion flakes, chicken broth, and bell pepper. Stir until well blended.

Place chicken breasts in small casserole dish sprayed with nonstick cooking spray. Pour cream cheese mixture over top and bake for 35 minutes at 350 degrees F. Serve over pasta or rice if desired.

Recipe makes 2 servings.

Each serving provides:

188	Calories	1.5 g	Fat
34.9 g	Protein	0.39 g	Saturated fat
6.9 g	Carbohydrate	74 mg	Cholesterol

Diabetic exchanges: Lean meat, $3^{1}/_{4}$; vegetable, $^{1}/_{2}$

Family Casserole

A real crowd pleaser!

Nonfat nonstick cooking spray
$^1/_2$ pound ground turkey breast
$^1/_2$ cup chopped onion
$^1/_2$ cup tomato sauce
$^1/_2$ teaspoon salt (optional)
Black pepper to taste
$^3/_4$ cup lowfat (1 percent) cottage cheese
$^1/_4$ cup chopped green pepper
3 tablespoons light cream cheese
2 tablespoons light sour cream
$1^1/_2$ cups cooked elbow macaroni, drained
$^1/_3$ cup grated fat-free mozzarella cheese

Preheat oven to 350 degrees F

Spray skillet with nonstick cooking spray. Brown turkey breast and onion. Add tomato sauce and seasonings. Simmer 7 to 8 minutes. In medium bowl, combine cottage cheese, green pepper, cream cheese, and sour cream. Mix thoroughly.

Spray 8-inch square glass baking dish with nonstick cooking spray. Cover bottom with macaroni. Add meat mixture. Pour cottage cheese mixture on next, and top with grated cheese. Bake uncovered at 350 degrees F for 30 to 40 minutes.

Recipe makes 4 servings.

Each serving provides:

230	Calories	3.6 g	Fat
26.4 g	Protein	2.02 g	Saturated fat
21.9 g	Carbohydrate	45 mg	Cholesterol

Diabetic exchanges: Starch, 1; lean meat, $2^1/_3$; vegetable, 1

Honey Mustard Chicken

One of Doris's personal favorites.

4 boneless, skinless chicken breasts (3 ounces each)
$^1/_2$ teaspoon onion powder
$^1/_2$ teaspoon garlic powder
Salt and pepper to taste
Nonfat nonstick cooking spray
$^1/_2$ cup fat-free chicken broth
2 tablespoons Dijon mustard
$^1/_2$ teaspoon Molly McButter dry butter flavor sprinkles*
2 tablespoons honey
$^1/_4$ teaspoon light soy sauce

*This can be found in small bottles in the baking supplies section of the market.

Season both sides of chicken breasts with onion powder, garlic powder, salt, and pepper. Place seasoned chicken breasts in skillet sprayed with nonstick cooking spray. Cook over medium-low heat until done and brown on both sides. Remove chicken from skillet and set aside. Add all remaining ingredients to skillet. Stir over low heat 2 to 3 minutes. Pour over chicken breasts and serve.

Recipe makes 4 servings.

Each serving provides:

139	Calories	1.6 g	Fat
20.4 g	Protein	0.28 g	Saturated fat
9.7 g	Carbohydrate	49 mg	Cholesterol

Diabetic exchanges: Starch, $^1/_8$; lean meat, $1^3/_4$; fruit, $^1/_2$

Orange-Almond Chicken

———❦———

Bursting with citrus flavor!

2 tablespoons frozen orange juice concentrate, thawed
$1/4$ teaspoon almond extract
$1/2$ teaspoon finely grated orange peel
$1/4$ cup crushed cornflakes
$1/3$ cup sliced almonds, chopped lightly
2 boneless, skinless chicken breasts (3 ounces each)
Nonfat nonstick cooking spray

In small bowl, combine orange juice concentrate, almond extract, and grated orange peel. Stir with spoon until thoroughly mixed.

In another small bowl, combine cornflakes and sliced almonds. Mix with spoon. Pour the mixture onto a small plate.

Marinate chicken breasts in orange juice mixture for 15 minutes. Roll in cornflakes and almonds.

Spray small skillet with nonstick cooking spray and place each chicken breast in skillet. Brown and cook over medium-low heat.

Recipe makes 2 servings.

Each serving provides:

276	Calories	11.2 g	Fat
24.6 g	Protein	1.28 g	Saturated fat
20.0 g	Carbohydrate	49 mg	Cholesterol

Diabetic exchanges: Starch, $3/4$; lean meat, $1^3/4$; fruit, $1/2$; fat, 2

Spicy Garlic Butter Shrimp

—❧—

This dish has a snappy flavor that's just wonderful.

Nonfat nonstick cooking spray
$^1\!/_2$ cup fat-free chicken broth
1 teaspoon Molly McButter dry butter flavor sprinkles*
2 cloves garlic, pressed
8 extra-large cooked and peeled shrimp
1 tablespoon fresh chopped parsley
$^1\!/_4$ teaspoon red pepper flakes (use more or less as desired)
$^1\!/_4$ fresh lemon (to squeeze)

Spray medium skillet with nonstick cooking spray. Pour
chicken broth in skillet; add butter flavor sprinkles and
garlic. Simmer over medium-low heat for 2 minutes. Add
shrimp and continue simmering another 2 minutes.
Remove from skillet and arrange on a plate. Add chopped
parsley and red pepper flakes. Squeeze lemon over entire
dish and serve.

Recipe makes 2 servings.

	Each serving provides:		
98	Calories	1.0 g	Fat
18.5 g	Protein	0.25 g	Saturated fat
2.5 g	Carbohydrate	166 mg	Cholesterol

Diabetic exchanges: Lean meat, $1^1\!/_2$; vegetable, $^1\!/_4$

---

*This can be found in small bottles in the baking supplies section of the
market.

Southwest White Chili

—❦—

Warms your tummy on a cold winter night.

Nonfat nonstick cooking spray
1 small onion, chopped
$^1/_2$ stalk celery, diced
1 boneless, skinless chicken breast (3 ounces),
    cut in small pieces
1 can (14$^1/_2$ ounces) fat-free chicken broth
1$^1/_4$ cups water
$^3/_4$ cup canned white beans
2 tablespoons chopped, canned green chilies
1 teaspoon chili powder
1 clove garlic, pressed
Salt and black pepper to taste
$^1/_4$ cup fat-free sour cream

Spray medium skillet with nonstick cooking spray. Add onion, celery, and chicken pieces and brown over medium heat.

In large pot, add all remaining ingredients except sour cream. Add browned onion, celery, and chicken. Simmer over low heat about 1 hour, or longer if desired. Stir in sour cream just before serving.

Recipe makes 4 servings.

Each serving provides:

113	Calories	0.6 g	Fat
10.9 g	Protein	0.14 g	Saturated fat
16.1 g	Carbohydrate	12 mg	Cholesterol

Diabetic exchanges: Starch, ½; lean meat, 1; vegetable, ½

Spicy Jalapeño Chicken Breasts

Guys love this recipe!

4 boneless, skinless chicken breasts (3 ounces each)
$1/3$ cup flour
Salt and black pepper to taste
Nonfat nonstick cooking spray
1 10-ounce can Rotel tomatoes
$1/2$ medium onion, chopped
1 tablespoon Tabasco jalapeño sauce (the green one)
1 fresh, sliced jalapeño pepper, seeds removed
1 clove garlic, pressed
$1/2$ cup fat-free chicken broth

Preheat oven to 350 degrees F

Dust each chicken breast on both sides with flour. Season each with salt and black pepper as desired. Place in skillet sprayed with nonstick cooking spray and brown on both sides.

Use a medium bowl to combine tomatoes, onion, Tabasco jalapeño sauce, sliced jalapeño pepper, garlic, and chicken broth. Mix with spoon.

Spray an 8- or 9-inch baking dish with nonstick cooking spray. Place browned chicken breasts in dish and cover with tomato and jalapeño mixture. Bake uncovered for 30 to 40 minutes.

Recipe makes 4 servings.

Each serving provides:

208	Calories	3.3 g	Fat
28.9 g	Protein	0.90 g	Saturated fat
13.6 g	Carbohydrate	73 mg	Cholesterol

Diabetic exchanges: Starch, $^1/_2$; lean meat, $2^1/_2$; vegetable, 1

Tex-Mex Burrito

—— ⚘ ——

Tastes great anytime, especially when you're in the mood for Mexican food.

Nonfat nonstick cooking spray
1 small onion, chopped
2 tablespoons canned, chopped green chilies
1 clove garlic, pressed
$\frac{1}{2}$ cup canned fat-free refried beans
Garlic salt to taste
Black pepper to taste
Cayenne pepper if desired
2 small fat-free flour tortillas
4 tablespoons fat-free sour cream
$\frac{1}{2}$ cup Kraft shredded fat-free cheese

In small skillet sprayed with nonstick cooking spray, brown onion and chopped green chilies. Stir over medium-low heat until onion is done. Add pressed garlic and stir until garlic is done (2 to 4 minutes).

Remove from heat and mix with refried beans. Add garlic salt, black pepper, and cayenne pepper. Stir until thoroughly mixed. Spread half of mixture on each tortilla and use half of the sour cream and shredded cheese on each tortilla. Roll flour tortilla up with mixture and serve.

Recipe makes 2 servings.

Each serving provides:

267	Calories	1.0 g	Fat
15.8 g	Protein	0.11 g	Saturated fat
52.1 g	Carbohydrate	0 mg	Cholesterol

Diabetic exchanges: Starch, 2½; lean meat, 1; vegetable, 1

Avocado and Cream Cheese Sandwich

Makes a light and refreshing summer lunch.

2 slices of lowfat bread, toasted
2 tablespoons fat-free cream cheese
Black pepper to taste
3 to 4 slices of avocado, sliced fairly thin
1 to 2 slices of onion, sliced thin
5 to 6 slices of fresh cucumber

Spread one side of toast with cream cheese and add black pepper on top of cream cheese. Begin layering all other sliced vegetables onto sandwich. Add top piece of toast. Slice in half and serve.

Recipe makes 2 servings.

Each serving provides:

105	Calories	4.4 g	Fat
4.7 g	Protein	0.70 g	Saturated fat
13.8 g	Carbohydrate	2 mg	Cholesterol

Diabetic exchanges: Starch, $\frac{1}{2}$; lean meat, $\frac{1}{4}$; vegetable, $\frac{1}{2}$; fat, $\frac{3}{4}$

Pepper Chicken

Deep, zesty flavor.

Nonfat nonstick cooking spray
2 boneless, skinless chicken breasts (4 ounces each)
$^1/_4$ teaspoon cayenne pepper, ground (optional)
$^1/_4$ teaspoon black pepper
Salt to taste
1 small onion, chopped
$^1/_4$ cup fresh green pepper, chopped

Spray small to medium skillet with nonstick cooking
spray. Season each side of chicken breast with cayenne
pepper, black pepper, and salt to taste, then brown in skillet. Add chopped onion and green pepper and simmer for
15 to 20 minutes over medium to low heat. Cover for the
first 5 minutes, then lightly stir over heat for the remaining time. Onion and green pepper should be lightly
browned.

Recipe makes 2 servings.

Each serving provides:

152	Calories	1.5 g	Fat
27.1 g	Protein	0.40 g	Saturated fat
6.7 g	Carbohydrate	65 mg	Cholesterol

Diabetic exchanges: Lean meat, $2^1/_4$; vegetable, 1

The Best Tortilla Casserole

The title says it all—delicious!

Nonfat nonstick cooking spray
$1/2$ cup canned fat-free refried beans
1 medium onion, chopped
$1/2$ pound ground turkey breast
$1/2$ package taco seasoning
$1/3$ cup water
$1/2$ can Campbell's 98-percent fat-free cream of
    mushroom soup
2 tablespoons canned, chopped green chilies
$1/4$ cup fat-free sour cream
$1/2$ cup grated fat-free Cheddar or American cheese
$1/2$ cup crushed baked tortilla chips

Preheat oven to 350 degrees F

Spray 9-inch glass baking dish lightly with nonstick cooking spray. Use refried beans and half of the chopped onion to cover bottom of the dish.

Brown ground turkey in skillet sprayed with nonstick cooking spray. Add taco seasoning and stir. Add water and cream of mushroom soup and green chilies. Add sour cream and remove from heat. Stir thoroughly. Pour this mixture over the beans in casserole dish. Add grated cheese and remaining chopped onion. Top with crushed tortilla chips. Bake at 350 degrees F for 25 to 30 minutes. Serve warm.

Recipe makes 6 servings.

Each serving provides:

157	Calories	1.3 g	Fat
15.1 g	Protein	0.31 g	Saturated fat
21.1 g	Carbohydrate	25 mg	Cholesterol

Diabetic exchanges: Starch, 1; lean meat, 1; vegetable, 2/3

Sour Cream Veggie Enchiladas

❧

These are sooooo good!

Nonfat nonstick cooking spray
$1/3$ cup fat-free chicken broth
1 fresh carrot, sliced
1 cup fresh sliced mushrooms
1 small yellow squash, sliced
1 stalk celery, chopped
1 small onion, sliced
6 thin slices of red, green, or yellow bell pepper
1 clove garlic, pressed
$1/4$ teaspoon garlic salt
1 small tomato, chopped
$1/2$ cup frozen corn, thawed
4 small fat-free flour tortillas

Topping
$1/2$ cup fat-free cottage cheese
$1/2$ cup fat-free shredded mozzarella cheese
1 green onion including top, chopped
$1/3$ cup fresh spinach, chopped
$1/2$ teaspoon garlic salt or powder
$1/2$ cup fat-free sour cream

Preheat oven to 350 degrees F

Spray large skillet with nonstick cooking spray. Add chicken broth and carrot. Simmer and stir over medium heat for 2 minutes. Add mushrooms and simmer 2 to 3 minutes. Add yellow squash, celery, onion, pepper slices, pressed garlic, and garlic salt. Add a little chicken broth or water if needed for moisture. Simmer and stir until vegetables are almost done. Add tomato and corn. Do not overcook; leave some crunch in the vegetables. Cool slightly.

Place about $1/2$ cup mixture on each tortilla and roll. Place each in 8- or 9-inch baking dish sprayed with nonstick cooking spray. Repeat until all flour tortillas are rolled.

Combine all topping ingredients in small bowl and mix. Pour the mixture over rolled tortillas.

Bake at 350 degrees F for 25 to 30 minutes.

Recipe makes 4 servings.

Each serving provides:

250	Calories	1.0 g	Fat
16.6 g	Protein	0.16 g	Saturated fat
44.7 g	Carbohydrate	5 mg	Cholesterol

Diabetic exchanges: Starch, $1^{1}/_{2}$; lean meat, $^{1}/_{2}$; vegetable, 2; skim milk, $^{3}/_{4}$

Veggie Quiche

Quick and easy—great for when you have company.

1 9-inch frozen regular Pet Ritz pie crust
1¼ cups fat-free liquid egg product
1 cup chopped fresh spinach
2 green onions, chopped
⅓ cup fat-free sour cream
1 teaspoon Molly McButter dry butter flavor sprinkles*
¼ cup grated raw carrot
½ cup canned sliced mushrooms
Salt and black pepper to taste
¼ cup Sargento light grated Cheddar cheese

*This can be found in small bottles in the baking supplies section of the market.

Preheat oven to 350 degrees F

While pie crust is still frozen, remove from aluminum pie plate and place in glass pie plate.

In large bowl, combine all remaining ingredients except cheese. Mix thoroughly and pour into unbaked pie shell. Sprinkle top with grated cheese and bake for about 40 minutes or until set.

Recipe makes 6 servings.

Each serving provides:

162	Calories	6.3 g	Fat
9.2 g	Protein	2.7 g	Saturated fat
16.2 g	Carbohydrate	6 mg	Cholesterol

Diabetic exchanges: Starch, 1; lean meat, 1; vegetable, 1

Pies, Pastries, and Desserts

Blackberries and Pudding

Sweet Almond Cake

Apple Cinnamon Sticks

Apple Cobbler

Warm Apple Turnovers

Apricot Turnovers

Banana Cream Pie

Carrot Cake with Cream Cheese Icing

Brownie Sour Cream Cake

Sweet Cherry Pockets

Cherry Upside-Down Cake

Cherry Chocolate Chip Pie

Cherry Cobbler

Cream Cheese Chocolate Sauce Dip

Chocolate Fudge Balls

Chocolate-Peanut Butter Cream Pie

Chocolate Cream Pie Supreme

Cherry Swirl Cake

Coconut Cream Pie

Cranberry-Orange Bundt Cake

Easy No-Bake Lemon Cheesecake
Lemon Chess Pie
Lemon Cookies and Cream Dessert
Peaches and Cream Dessert
Lemon Sour Cream Cake with Cream Cheese Frosting
Orange-Apricot Coffee Cake
Orange Poppy Seed Cake
Peanut Butter Pie
Peach Pockets
Pineapple Upside-Down Cake
Deluxe Pineapple Cream Pie
Pineapple Cream Pie
Creamy Pistachio Dessert
Raspberry Coffee Cake
Pumpkin Pie Deluxe
Pumpkin Squares with Orange Cream Cheese Icing
Raspberry Sweet Rollers
Pineapple Cream Cake
Chocolate Silk Pie
Tropical Fruit Pie
Chocolate Mousse Cheesecake
Chocolate Banana Cream Dessert
Chocolate Cake with Fudge Frosting

Blackberries and Pudding

Absolutely divine! When the rest of your family is hogging down some evil dessert, fix this quickie for yourself. You'll love it!

1/2 cup frozen blackberries
2 tablespoons water
2 teaspoons vanilla sugar-free instant pudding mix
Equal sweetener

Place frozen blackberries in bowl, add water, and thaw in microwave. Do not allow berries to get hot. Remove from microwave and stir. Add instant pudding mix, and sweetener if desired, and stir with spoon until mixed thoroughly. Serve and enjoy.

Recipe makes 1 serving.

Each serving provides:

66	Calories	0.4 g	Fat
0.7 g	Protein	0.01 g	Saturated fat
16.5 g	Carbohydrate	0 mg	Cholesterol

Diabetic exchange: fruit, 1

Sweet Almond Cake

This cake has the wonderful, delicate almond flavor that we adore. It can be served as a breakfast cake or a dessert.

Nonfat nonstick cooking spray
2 cups reduced-fat Bisquick baking mix
1 1/4 cups skim milk
1/4 cup sugar
1 1/2 teaspoons vanilla
1/2 cup fat-free sour cream
1 1/2 teaspoons almond extract
1 teaspoon Molly McButter butter flavor sprinkles*
3 packets Sweet 'n Low sweetener
2 teaspoons Brown Sugar Twin, reserve for top of batter
1/3 cup sliced almonds, reserve for top of batter
2 tablespoons Equal sweetener, reserve for top of baked cake

*This can be found in small bottles in the baking supplies section of the market.

Preheat oven to 350 degrees F

Spray 8-inch square baking dish with nonstick cooking spray. In large bowl, combine baking mix, skim milk, sugar, vanilla, sour cream, almond extract, butter flavor sprinkles, and Sweet 'n Low sweetener. Use an electric mixer and mix thoroughly. Pour batter into baking dish. Sprinkle 2 teaspoons Brown Sugar Twin on top of batter. Sprinkle sliced almonds evenly over top. Bake at 350 degrees F for 40 minutes. After cake has cooled a little, sprinkle on Equal sweetener.

Recipe makes 9 servings.

Each serving provides:

184	Calories	4.0 g	Fat
7.9 g	Protein	0.60 g	Saturated fat
28.8 g	Carbohydrate	1 mg	Cholesterol

Diabetic exchanges: Starch, 2; skim milk, ¼

Apple Cinnamon Sticks

—❧—

Go ahead and double this recipe because these will get eaten in a hurry! Just the apple-cinnamon smell coming from the oven will have people gathering in the kitchen whether you want them there or not.

Nonfat nonstick butter-flavored cooking spray
4 eggroll wrappers*
4 tablespoons unsweetened applesauce
4 tablespoons Equal sweetener
2 teaspoons Molly McButter butter flavor sprinkles**
Cinnamon

Preheat oven to 400 degrees F

Spray small baking sheet with cooking spray. Use a dinner plate as a work surface for the eggroll wrappers. Place one wrapper on the plate. Spread 1 tablespoon applesauce

*These are usually found in the produce section of the market.

**This can be found in small bottles in the baking supplies section of the market.

on wrapper surface. Sprinkle 1 tablespoon Equal, ½ teaspoon butter flavor sprinkles, and a little cinnamon over applesauce. Start at one corner and roll up like a pencil. Place on baking sheet and repeat process for other eggroll wrappers. Spray tops of each stick with cooking spray. Bake at 400 degrees F for 9 minutes.

Recipe makes 4 sticks. One serving equals 2 sticks.

Each serving provides:

272	Calories	0.0 g	Fat
29.8 g	Protein	0.00 g	Saturated fat
38.9 g	Carbohydrate	0 mg	Cholesterol

Diabetic exchanges: Starch, 2; fruit, 2

Apple Cobbler

—❧—

One of our favorites. . . . Very yummy!

Filling
1 can (20 ounces) sliced apples in water, do not drain
$^1/_3$ cup frozen apple juice concentrate, thawed
1 teaspoon cinnamon
$^1/_4$ teaspoon Molly McButter dry butter flavor sprinkles*
$^1/_2$ teaspoon vanilla

Crust
1 $^1/_3$ cups reduced-fat Bisquick baking mix
1 cup evaporated fat-free skim milk
1 tablespoon frozen apple juice concentrate, thawed
$^1/_2$ teaspoon vanilla
Nonfat nonstick cooking spray
2 tablespoons Equal sweetener, to sprinkle on top after
    baking

Preheat oven to 350 degrees F
In medium bowl, combine apples in water, $^1/_3$ cup apple
juice concentrate, cinnamon, butter flavor sprinkles, and
vanilla, and stir with spoon. In another medium bowl,
combine baking mix, skim milk, 1 tablespoon apple juice

*This can be found in small bottles in the baking supplies section of the market.

concentrate, and vanilla and stir. Batter will be somewhat thin. Spray 8 × 8-inch baking dish with cooking spray and pour half the crust batter into it. Spoon filling mixture onto batter. Pour remaining batter over top, though it will not completely cover filling. Do not worry, it will cook and look just fine! Bake cobbler at 350 degrees F for 35 to 40 minutes. When done cooking, sprinkle Equal sweetener over top of cobbler.

Recipe makes 9 servings.

Each serving provides:

143	Calories	1.4 g	Fat
6.3 g	Protein	0.29 g	Saturated fat
25.9 g	Carbohydrate	1 mg	Cholesterol

Diabetic exchanges: Starch, 1; fat, ¼; fruit, 1

Warm Apple Turnovers

Marvelous on a cold winter day, and a real treat for breakfast.

Turnovers
Nonfat nonstick cooking spray
6 packets Sweet 'n Low sweetener
$^1/_2$ teaspoon Molly McButter dry butter flavor sprinkles*
1 teaspoon cinnamon
1 can (20 ounces) sliced apples in water, do not drain
8 eggroll wrappers**
1 egg white, slightly beaten

Sprinkle Topping
3 tablespoons Equal
$^1/_2$ teaspoon cinnamon

Preheat oven to 350 degrees F

Spray baking sheet with cooking spray. In medium bowl, combine Sweet 'n Low sweetner, butter flavor sprinkles, and 1 teaspoon cinnamon, and mix with spoon. Add sliced apples with their water and stir with spoon until well mixed. Take an eggroll wrapper and dip one side in egg

*This can be found in small bottles in the baking supplies section of the market.

**These are usually found in the produce section of the market.

white. Place dipped side down on large plate. Place about
$^1/_3$ cup apple mixture in center of eggroll wrapper. Take
edge closest to you and fold toward center halfway. Fold
left and right edges into center and finish rolling. Place on
baking sheet and repeat procedure for remaining wrappers. Bake at 350 degrees F for 35 minutes. While
turnovers are baking, combine Equal sweetener and cinnamon for topping. Remove turnovers from oven and
sprinkle tops with cinnamon mixture. Serve warm.

Recipe makes 8 turnovers. One serving equals 1 turnover.

Each serving provides:

129	Calories	0.2 g	Fat
8.0 g	Protein	0.04 g	Saturated fat
24.7 g	Carbohydrate	0 mg	Cholesterol

Diabetic exchanges: Fruit, 1; starch, $^3/_4$

Apricot Turnovers

—— ✲ ——

If you want, you can pretend this is a fried pie. One thing for certain, it is delicious!

Nonfat nonstick butter-flavored cooking spray
1 can (15 ounces) light apricot halves, well drained and
    cut in quarters
1 teaspoon Molly McButter dry butter flavor sprinkles*
$^1/_2$ teaspoon vanilla
4 tablespoons Equal sweetener
$1^1/_2$ tablespoons cornstarch
Dash of cinnamon
4 eggroll wrappers**

Preheat oven to 400 degrees F

Spray baking sheet with cooking spray. In medium bowl, combine apricots, butter flavor sprinkles, vanilla, sweetener, cornstarch, and dash of cinnamon. Stir with spoon until cornstarch is dissolved. Using large dinner plate as work surface, place one eggroll wrapper on plate and

*This can be found in small bottles in the baking supplies section of the market.

**These are usually found in the produce section of the market.

spoon one-quarter of apricot mixture onto center. Bring bottom corner up and over apricot mixture. Roll and fold like small package. Seal final flap with drop of water and place sealed side up on baking sheet. Repeat procedure for remaining wrappers. Spray tops with cooking spray. Bake at 400 degrees F for 14 minutes.

Recipe makes 4 servings.

Each serving provides:

174	Calories	0.0 g	Fat
15.3 g	Protein	0.00 g	Saturated fat
28.9 g	Carbohydrate	0 mg	Cholesterol

Diabetic exchanges: Starch, 1; fruit, 1½

Banana Cream Pie

❦

Banana pie is a big favorite with so many people that you'll make this one again and again. It is fantastic! Note: For best results, serve this pie on the same day it is made. Most cream pies, including this one, deteriorate in appearance after the first day.

Pie
1 box (1.2 ounces) Jell-O sugar-free vanilla cook-and-serve pudding and pie filling
2½ cups skim milk
1 tub (8 ounces) fat-free cream cheese
4 tablespoons Equal sweetener
1 teaspoon vanilla
3 medium or 2 large ripe bananas, sliced
1 baked and cooled pie crust*

Topping
1 tub (8 ounces) fat-free cream cheese
1 teaspoon vanilla
4 tablespoons Equal sweetener

*We like Pillsbury Pet Ritz frozen pie crusts, which are quick and easy and have only 4 grams of fat per serving. If you do not want to use a frozen pie crust, you can use a mixture of ⅓ cup graham cracker crumbs and 1 tablespoon Equal, sprinkled on bottom of pie plate. This lowers fat per serving by 2 grams.

In medium bowl, combine pudding mix and milk. Cook as instructed on box. Set aside to cool for approximately 5 to 10 minutes. Stir a few times during cooling. In another medium bowl, combine cream cheese, Equal, and vanilla. Mix with electric mixer until smooth. Add cooled pudding and stir with spoon until thoroughly blended. Fold in sliced bananas. Pour into baked pie shell and chill until set, 1 to 2 hours.

While pie chills, combine cream cheese, vanilla, and sweetener. Mix with electric mixer until smooth. Spread over top of chilled pie. Return to refrigerator until ready to serve.

Recipe makes 8 servings.

Each serving provides:

261	Calories	4.4 g	Fat
24.1 g	Protein	1.67 g	Saturated fat
28.4 g	Carbohydrate	14 mg	Cholesterol

Diabetic exchanges: Starch, 2; fat, 1½

Carrot Cake
with Cream Cheese Icing

One of Doris's favorites!

Cake
1 cup cake flour
1 1/2 teaspoons baking powder
1/2 cup Equal sweetener
1/4 teaspoon Sweet 'n Low sweetener
1 1/2 tablespoons buttermilk powder
1/4 cup sugar
2 tablespoons margarine
1/4 cup fat-free liquid egg product
1/3 cup skim milk
3 tablespoons fat-free sour cream
1 cup fine grated carrots
2 teaspoons vanilla
2 1/2 teaspoons cinnamon
1/8 teaspoon ground cloves
Nonfat nonstick cooking spray

Cream Cheese Icing
1 tub (8 ounces) fat-free cream cheese
1/4 cup Equal sweetener
1 teaspoon vanilla
1/2 teaspoon Molly McButter butter flavor sprinkles*
1/4 cup fine chopped pecans, optional

*This can be found in small bottles in the baking supplies section of the market.

Preheat oven to 350 degrees F

In large bowl, combine cake flour, baking powder, Equal and Sweet 'n Low sweeteners, buttermilk powder, and sugar, and blend with spoon. Add margarine, egg product, skim milk, sour cream, carrots, vanilla, cinnamon, and cloves, and mix with electric mixer until thoroughly blended. Spray 9-inch square baking dish with cooking spray. Pour cake batter into baking dish and bake at 350 degrees F for 35 minutes. Test center of cake with tooth-pick to check for doneness. Remove and cool before icing.

In medium bowl, combine cream cheese, Equal sweetener, vanilla, and butter flavor sprinkles, and beat with electric mixer until smooth. Stir in pecans, if you wish. Pour and spread icing over cooled cake.

Recipe makes 9 servings.

Each serving provides:

198	Calories	2.8 g	Fat
22.3 g	Protein	0.74 g	Saturated fat
19.2 g	Carbohydrate	5 mg	Cholesterol

Diabetic exchanges: Lean protein, 1; starch, 1½; vegetable, 1

Brownie Sour Cream Cake

—❦—

Are you longing for something filled with chocolate?
Make this fantastic cake and indulge your cravings!

1 box (8½ ounces) Estee light chocolate cake mix*
¾ cup fat-free sour cream
⅓ cup Equal sweetener
1 teaspoon vanilla
1 egg white
½ cup plus 1 tablespoon water
Nonfat nonstick cooking spray
¼ cup mini chocolate chips

Preheat oven to 350 degrees F

In large bowl, combine cake mix, sour cream, sweetner,
vanilla, egg white, and water. Mix with electric mixer until
smooth. Spray 8-inch square glass baking dish with cooking
spray. Pour batter into baking dish and sprinkle with mini
chocolate chips. Bake at 350 degrees F for 30 to 35 minutes.
Test center of cake with toothpick to check for doneness.

Recipe makes 12 servings.

Each serving provides:

125	Calories	2.2 g	Fat
7.5 g	Protein	1.15 g	Saturated fat
18.3 g	Carbohydrate	0 mg	Cholesterol

Diabetic exchanges: Fat, ½; starch, 1¼

---

*Estee cake mixes are sweetened with fructose, not an artificial sweetener.
Consequently they are still fairly high in carbohydrates.

Sweet Cherry Pockets

$\mathscr{C}$

Delicious for snacks!

Nonfat nonstick cooking spray
3/4 cup pitted dark sweet cherries, well drained
1/2 teaspoon vanilla
3 tablespoons Equal sweetener
2 tablespoons graham cracker crumbs
4 eggroll wrappers*

Preheat oven to 400 degrees

Spray medium baking sheet with cooking spray. After draining cherries, place on paper towel. Press lightly to remove more juice. In medium bowl, combine vanilla, sweetener, graham cracker crumbs, and cherries, and mix thoroughly. Using large dinner plate for work surface, place an eggroll wrapper on plate and spoon one-fourth of mixture onto center. Fold wrapper edge to center and fold up sides like a package. Seal final flap with drop of water. Place on baking sheet with sealed side up. Repeat procedure for remaining wrappers. Spray tops with cooking spray. Bake at 400 degrees F for 13 to 14 minutes.

Recipe makes 4 servings.

Each serving provides:

150	Calories	0.5 g	Fat
12.5 g	Protein	0.13 g	Saturated fat
24.7 g	Carbohydrate	0 mg	Cholesterol

Diabetic exchanges: Starch, 1 1/2; fruit, 1/2

---

*These are usually found in the produce section of the market.

Cherry Upside-Down Cake

—✻—

This is luscious! Doris created this recipe after hearing about a much more fattening version. We were delighted with the results.

Cherry Layer
Nonfat nonstick cooking spray
1 can (16 ounces) tart red pitted cherries in water
3 tablespoons liquid from drained cherries, discard
    the rest
$^1/_3$ cup Equal sweetener
$^1/_2$ teaspoon Sweet 'n Low sweetener
$^1/_2$ teaspoon Molly McButter dry butter flavor sprinkles*
$^1/_4$ teaspoon almond extract

Cake
1 cup cake flour
1 $^1/_2$ teaspoons baking powder
$^1/_2$ cup Equal sweetener
$^1/_2$ teaspoon Sweet 'n Low sweetener
1 tablespoon powdered buttermilk
2 tablespoons margarine
$^1/_4$ cup fat-free liquid egg product
$^1/_4$ cup sugar
$^1/_3$ cup skim milk
1 $^1/_2$ teaspoons vanilla
1 $^1/_2$ teaspoons almond extract

*This can be found in small bottles in the baking supplies section of the market.

Preheat oven to 350 degrees F

Spray 8-inch square glass baking dish with cooking spray. In small bowl, combine cherries, 3 tablespoons cherry liquid, sweeteners, butter flavor sprinkles, and almond extract, and stir with spoon. Pour into bottom of baking dish and spread evenly.

In medium bowl, combine cake flour, baking powder, sweeteners, powdered buttermilk, and mix with a spoon. In another medium bowl combine margarine, egg product, sugar, skim milk, vanilla, and almond extract, and beat with electric mixer. Add dry ingredients and mix thoroughly with electric mixer. Pour batter over cherry mixture in baking dish. Bake at 350 degrees F for 35 to 40 minutes. Cool and serve.

Note: We do not turn out our cake upside down, however you can, if desired.

Recipe makes 9 servings.

Each serving provides:

185	Calories	2.8 g	Fat
20.3 g	Protein	0.74 g	Saturated fat
19.7 g	Carbohydrate	1 mg	Cholesterol

Diabetic exchanges: Fruit, 1; starch, 1½

Cherry Chocolate Chip Pie

———— ✄ ————

If you like cherry and chocolate together, here's a dessert you're bound to love! Alice was marked by a childhood experience of eating some dreadful cherry-chocolate candy bar, so it was up to Doris to declare this recipe "mighty yummy."

Pie

1 can (16 ounces) tart red pitted cherries packed in water, drain and retain juice
2 tablespoons cornstarch
1 teaspoon Molly McButter butter flavor sprinkles*
1 teaspoon vanilla
1/2 teaspoon almond extract
1/4 teaspoon Sweet 'n Low sweetener
3/4 cup Equal sweetener
1/4 cup mini chocolate chips
1 (9-inch) frozen pie crust, baked and cooled**

Topping

1 tub (8 ounces) fat-free cream cheese
1/4 cup Equal sweetener
1 teaspoon vanilla
2 tablespoons skim milk

*This can be found in small bottles in the baking supplies section of the market.

**We like Pillsbury Pet Ritz frozen pie crusts, which are quick and easy and have only 4 grams of fat per serving. If you do not want to use a frozen pie crust, use 1/3 cup graham cracker crumbs mixed with 1 tablespoon Equal sprinkled on bottom of pie plate. This will lower the grams of fat per serving.

In medium saucepan, combine juice from cherries, cornstarch, butter flavor sprinkles, vanilla, almond extract, and Sweet 'n Low sweetener. Stir constantly over medium heat until juice thickens. Remove from heat and add cherries and Equal sweetener, and stir to mix. Cool this mixture for about 20 minutes, stirring occasionally. Add mini chocolate chips and stir to mix. Pour mixture into baked pie shell and set aside to cool further.

In medium bowl, mix cream cheese, sweetener, and vanilla, and mix with electric mixer until smooth. Add skim milk and beat again. Pour over top of cherry filling and gently spread to cover. Serve at room temperature. Store remaining pie in refrigerator.

Recipe makes 8 servings.

Each serving provides:

208	Calories	6.6 g	Fat
11.8 g	Protein	2.92 g	Saturated fat
23.6 g	Carbohydrate	8 mg	Cholesterol

Diabetic exchanges: Fat, 1; fruit, 1; starch, 1¼

Cherry Cobbler

———✦———

We just can't think of anything finer than cherry cobbler.
Except maybe cherry cobbler with ice cream.

Filling
1 can (16 ounces) tart red pitted cherries packed in water
15 packets Sweet One or Sweet 'n Low sweetener
1/2 teaspoon Molly McButter dry butter flavor sprinkles*
1 teaspoon vanilla

Crust
1 1/3 cups reduced-fat Bisquick baking mix
1 cup canned fat-free evaporated skim milk
2 packets Sweet One or Sweet 'n Low sweetener
1/2 teaspoon vanilla
Nonfat nonstick cooking spray

Preheat oven to 350 degrees F

In medium bowl, combine cherries and their juice,
sweetener, butter flavor sprinkles, and vanilla, and mix
with spoon.

*This can be found in small bottles in the baking supplies section of the market.

In another medium bowl, combine baking mix, skim milk, sweetener, and vanilla, and mix with spoon. Spray an 8-inch square baking dish with cooking spray. Pour half of batter into bottom of baking dish. Spoon cherry filling on top. Pour remaining batter over filling. There will not be enough batter to completely cover the top, but it will bake and look fine. Bake cobbler at 350 degrees F for 35 to 40 minutes.

Recipe makes 9 servings.

Each serving provides:

131	Calories	1.2 g	Fat
3.8 g	Protein	0.27 g	Saturated fat
26.2 g	Carbohydrate	1 mg	Cholesterol

Diabetic exchanges: Fruit, 1; starch, 1

Cream Cheese Chocolate Sauce Dip

Wonderful sweet treat for a party! Use as a dip with fresh strawberries, chunks of banana, or angel food cake torn into small chunks.

2 tablespoons fat-free sugar-free chocolate ice cream
    topping
4 tablespoons fat-free cream cheese
3 tablespoons Equal sweetener

Stir all ingredients together in a small bowl. Mix until smooth and creamy.

Note: If you make this for a party or small gathering, you will need to double or triple the recipe.

Recipe makes 2 servings.

Each serving provides:

142	Calories	0.0 g	Fat
23.0 g	Protein	0.00 g	Saturated fat
11.0 g	Carbohydrate	6 mg	Cholesterol

Diabetic exchanges: Starch, 1; lean protein, 1

Chocolate Fudge Balls

—✦—

Rich and wonderful! (Doris is an admitted chocolate addict and came up with this recipe while under the influence of a "chocolate frenzy.")

1 tub (8 ounces) fat-free cream cheese
$^1\!/_2$ teaspoon vanilla
$^1\!/_3$ cup Equal sweetener
1 envelope (1$^1\!/_2$ ounces) Sans Sucre sugar-free lowfat
    chocolate mousse mix
$^3\!/_4$ cup Cocoa Pebbles cereal
$^3\!/_4$ cup uncooked oatmeal*

Using electric mixer, beat cream cheese until smooth. Add vanilla and sweetener, and continue mixing. Add chocolate mousse mix and blend. When thoroughly mixed, stir in Cocoa Pebbles with spoon.

    Place oatmeal in small bowl. Drop walnut size spoonfuls of chocolate mixture into oatmeal to cover outside of each ball. Place on wax paper or on dish and serve. Store in refrigerator.

Recipe makes 16 walnut-size balls. One serving equals 2 balls.

Each serving provides:

127	Calories	1.9 g	Fat
13.4 g	Protein	0.64 g	Saturated fat
12.3 g	Carbohydrate	5 mg	Cholesterol

Diabetic exchanges: Starch, 1; lean protein, 1

---

*Oatmeal is for coating outside of balls. Though you will not use all of $^3\!/_4$ cup, you will need this much to work with.

Chocolate-Peanut Butter Cream Pie

Chocolate and peanut butter together! Yes, yes, yes! As with other cream pies, this pie is best when served the same day. Its appearance deteriorates after the first day.

Pie
1 package (2 ounces) Jell-O sugar-free chocolate cook-
    and-serve pudding and pie filling
2 1/2 cups skim milk
1 tub (8 ounces) fat-free cream cheese
1 teaspoon vanilla
4 tablespoons Equal sweetener
1 baked and cooled pie crust*

Topping
1 tub (8 ounces) fat-free cream cheese
2 tablespoons smooth peanut butter
1 teaspoon vanilla
4 tablespoons Equal sweetener

In medium bowl, combine pudding mix and milk, and cook in microwave or on stove top according to package. Set aside to cool, stirring a few times while cooling.

---

*We like Pillsbury Pet Ritz frozen pie crusts. They are quick and easy and have only 4 grams of fat per serving. If you do not want to use a frozen pie crust, use 1/3 cup graham cracker crumbs mixed with 1 tablespoon Equal, sprinkled on bottom of pie plate. This will lower the fat by 2 grams per serving.

In another medium bowl, combine cream cheese, vanilla, and sweetener. Mix with electric mixer until smooth. Add to pudding and stir with spoon until blended. Pour into baked pie shell. Chill for 1 to 2 hours.

While pie chills, combine cream cheese, peanut butter, vanilla, and sweetener, and mix with electric mixer until smooth. After pie has set, gently spread topping over top. Chill until ready to serve.

Recipe makes 8 servings.

Each serving provides:

252	Calories	6.3 g	Fat
24.7 g	Protein	1.99 g	Saturated fat
20.7 g	Carbohydrate	14 mg	Cholesterol

Diabetic exchanges: Skim milk, 1; lean protein, 1½; starch, 1

Chocolate Cream Pie Supreme

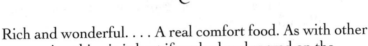

Rich and wonderful. . . . A real comfort food. As with other cream pies, this pie is best if cooked and served on the same day. The appearance deteriorates after the first day.

Pie
2½ cups skim milk
1 package (2 ounces) Jell-O sugar-free chocolate cook-and-serve pudding and pie filling
1 tub (8 ounces) fat-free cream cheese
1 teaspoon vanilla
4 tablespoons Equal sweetener
1 baked and cooled pie crust*

Topping
1 tub (8 ounces) fat-free cream cheese
1 teaspoon vanilla
4 tablespoons Equal sweetener

In medium bowl, combine milk and pudding mix, and cook in microwave or stove top following cooking times on package. When pudding is done, set aside to cool. Stir

*We like Pillsbury Pet Ritz frozen pie crusts. They are quick and easy and have only 4 grams of fat per serving. If you do not want to use the frozen pie crust, use ⅓ cup graham cracker crumbs mixed with 1 tablespoon Equal, sprinkled on bottom of pie plate. This will lower fat by 2 grams per serving.

a few times while cooling. In another medium bowl, combine cream cheese, vanilla, and sweetener. Mix with electric mixer until smooth. Combine this mixture with pudding mix and pour into pie shell. Chill for 1-2 hours.

While pie is chilling, combine topping ingredients and mix with electric mixer until smooth. Spread topping over chilled pie and return to refrigerator to finish chilling and setting.

Recipe makes 8 servings.

Each serving provides:

228	Calories	4.2 g	Fat
23.7 g	Protein	1.59 g	Saturated fat
19.9 g	Carbohydrate	14 mg	Cholesterol

Diabetic exchanges: Starch, 1^1/$_3$; lean protein, 2^1/$_2$

Cherry Swirl Cake

One of Doris's favorites!

Cherry Swirl
1 can (16 ounces) tart red pitted cherries packed in water
$^1/_3$ cup liquid from cherries
$^1/_2$ teaspoon Sweet 'n Low sweetener
$^1/_2$ teaspoon Molly McButter dry butter flavor sprinkles*
2 tablespoons cornstarch
$^1/_3$ cup Equal sweetener
1 teaspoon almond extract

Cake
1 cup cake flour
1 $^1/_2$ teaspoons baking powder
$^1/_2$ cup Equal sweetener
$^1/_2$ teaspoon Sweet 'n Low sweetener
1 tablespoon powdered buttermilk
$^1/_4$ cup sugar
$^1/_4$ cup fat-free sour cream
$^1/_2$ stick margarine ($^1/_4$ cup), softened slightly
$^1/_4$ cup fat-free liquid egg product
$^1/_4$ cup skim milk
1 $^1/_2$ teaspoons vanilla
1 teaspoon almond extract
Nonfat nonstick cooking spray

*This can be found in small bottles in the baking supplies section of the market.

Preheat oven to 350 degrees F

In medium saucepan, combine juice from cherries, Sweet 'n Low sweetener, butter flavor sprinkles, and cornstarch. Stir constantly over medium-low heat until juice starts to thicken. Remove from heat and add Equal sweetener, almond extract, and cherries, and stir with a spoon to mix.

In large bowl, combine flour, baking powder, sweeteners, and powdered buttermilk. Mix with spoon. Add sugar, sour cream, margarine, egg product, skim milk, vanilla, and almond extract, and mix with electric mixer until blended. Pour cherry swirl into bowl with batter and stir only a couple of times with spoon. Do not thoroughly mix cherries with batter. Spray 8-inch square baking dish with cooking spray. Pour entire mixture into baking dish and bake at 350 degrees F for 35 to 40 minutes. Test center with toothpick to see if it is done. Cool and serve.

Recipe makes 9 servings.

Each serving provides:

223	Calories	5.3 g	Fat
20.8 g	Protein	1.40 g	Saturated fat
23.2 g	Carbohydrate	1 mg	Cholesterol

Diabetic exchanges: Fruit, 1; starch, 1^1/$_2$; fat, 1

Coconut Cream Pie

—✤—

Since we both have southern accents, we feel qualified to speak about pies. . . . Especially cream pies. We crown this one the Champion! As with any cream pie, this is best if served the same day it is cooked. The appearance deteriorates after the first day.

Pie
1 box (1.2 ounces) Jell-O sugar-free vanilla cook-and-serve pudding and pie filling
2½ cups skim milk
1 tub (8 ounces) fat-free cream cheese
4 tablespoons Equal sweetener
1 teaspoon vanilla
½ teaspoon coconut extract
2 tablespoons flake coconut
1 baked and cooled pie crust*

Topping
1 tub (8 ounces) fat-free cream cheese
1 teaspoon vanilla
4 tablespoons Equal sweetener
⅛ teaspoon coconut extract
1 tablespoon flake coconut

*We like Pillsbury Pet Ritz frozen pie crusts. Quick and easy to use and only 4 grams of fat per serving. If you do not want to use a frozen pie crust, use ⅓ cup graham cracker crumbs mixed with 1 tablespoon Equal, sprinkled on bottom of pie plate. This will lower the grams of fat per serving.

In medium bowl, combine pudding mix and milk. Cook in microwave or on stove top following directions on box. Set aside to cool. Stir a few times while cooling.

In another medium bowl, combine cream cheese, sweetener, vanilla, coconut extract, and flake coconut. Use an electric mixer and mix until smooth. Combine this mixture with the pudding mixture and stir gently until mixed. Pour into baked pie shell and chill for 1 to 2 hours.

While pie chills, combine all ingredients for topping except flake coconut. Blend with electric mixer until smooth. Spread this mixture over top of chilled pie, sprinkle with coconut, and refrigerate until ready to serve.

Recipe makes 8 servings.

Each serving provides:

235	Calories	5.2 g	Fat
23.7 g	Protein	2.47 g	Saturated fat
19.2 g	Carbohydrate	14 mg	Cholesterol

Diabetic exchanges: Skim milk, 1; starch, 1^1/$_2$; fat, ^{1}/$_2$

Cranberry-Orange Bundt Cake

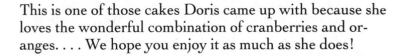

This is one of those cakes Doris came up with because she loves the wonderful combination of cranberries and oranges. . . . We hope you enjoy it as much as she does!

Cake
¼ cup dried cranberries, or fresh if available, grated
½ cup skim milk
½ cup unsweetened applesauce
2½ cups reduced-fat Bisquick baking mix
1½ teaspoons vanilla
½ teaspoon orange extract
⅓ cup fat-free liquid egg product
½ cup Equal sweetener
4 packets Sweet 'n Low sweetener
Grated peel from 1 medium orange
Nonfat nonstick cooking spray

Orange Glaze
⅓ cup frozen orange juice concentrate, thawed
2 tablespoons Equal sweetener
¼ teaspoon vanilla
¼ teaspoon Molly McButter dry butter flavor sprinkles*

*This can be found in small bottles in the baking supplies section of the market.

Preheat oven to 375 degrees F

In food processor, combine cranberries, milk, and apple-sauce. Process for 30 seconds and then let stand 5 minutes. In large bowl, combine processed mixture with baking mix, vanilla, orange extract, egg product, sweeteners, and grated orange peel. Stir by hand until thoroughly mixed. Spray bundt pan with cooking spray. Place dough evenly around the bundt pan and bake at 375 degrees F for 30 minutes. Cool cake and remove from pan.

In small bowl, combine all ingredients for glaze. After cake has cooled, spoon glaze over top of cake.

Recipe makes 10 servings.

Each serving provides:

218	Calories	2.0 g	Fat
15.7 g	Protein	0.40 g	Saturated fat
33.5 g	Carbohydrate	0 mg	Cholesterol

Diabetic exchanges: Fruit, 1; starch, 2

Easy No-Bake
Lemon Cheesecake

This is so refreshing on a hot day, and so simple to make!

Crust
Nonfat nonstick cooking spray
$^{1}/_{3}$ cup graham cracker crumbs
1 tablespoon Equal sweetener
$^{1}/_{4}$ teaspoon Molly McButter dry butter flavor sprinkles*

Filling
1 box (0.3 ounces) sugar-free lemon Jell-O
$^{1}/_{2}$ cup boiling water
1 tub (12 ounces) fat-free cream cheese
1 tub (8 ounces) fat-free cream cheese
1 cup fat-free sour cream
1 teaspoon vanilla
$^{3}/_{4}$ cup Equal sweetener
Grated peel from 1 lemon

Spray 9-inch pie plate with cooking spray. In small bowl, combine graham cracker crumbs, sweetener, and butter flavor sprinkles, and stir with spoon. Sprinkle crust mixture evenly over bottom of pie plate.

*This can be found in small bottles in the baking supplies section of the market.

In small bowl, dissolve Jell-O in boiling water. Stir until thoroughly dissolved.

In large bowl, mix cream cheese with electric mixer until smooth. Beat in sour cream. Add vanilla, sweetener, grated lemon peel, and Jell-O. Mix until smooth. Gently pour filling into pie plate, trying not to disturb graham cracker crumbs. Chill for a few hours and serve.

Recipe makes 8 servings.

Each serving provides:

182	Calories	0.4 g	Fat
32.6 g	Protein	0.11 g	Saturated fat
8.7 g	Carbohydrate	13 mg	Cholesterol

Diabetic exchanges: Starch, $^1/_2$; lean protein, 4

Lemon Chess Pie

———— ✦ ————

An old-fashioned pie with a lovely fresh lemon taste! If you had a little southern grandma, she would probably want you to have a second piece so you won't "waste away."

1 cup fat-free liquid egg product
$^3/_4$ cup canned evaporated skim milk
$^1/_4$ cup flour
1 tablespoon cornmeal
1 $^1/_2$ teaspoons vanilla
$^1/_4$ cup lemon juice
$^1/_2$ teaspoon lemon extract
$^1/_4$ teaspoon Sweet 'n Low sweetener
$^1/_2$ cup Equal sweetener
$^1/_4$ cup fat-free sour cream
1 9-inch frozen pie crust*
2 tablespoons Equal sweetener, for top after baking

*We like Pillsbury Pet Ritz frozen pie crusts. Quick and easy to use and only 4 grams of fat per serving. It helps to remove pie crust from foil pan while still frozen. If you do not want to use a frozen pie crust, use $^1/_3$ cup graham cracker crumbs mixed with 1 tablespoon Equal, sprinkled on bottom of pie plate. This will lower the grams of fat per serving.

Preheat oven to 350 degrees F

In large bowl, combine all ingredients except 2 table-spoons Equal for top after baking. Use electric mixer and blend until smooth. Pour filling into unbaked pie crust and bake at 350 degrees F for 35 minutes. Test center of pie with knife to test for doneness. If it comes out clean, it is done. Let pie cool about 10 or 15 minutes and then sprinkle on Equal.

Recipe makes 8 servings.

Each serving provides:

199	Calories	4.1 g	Fat
21.3 g	Protein	1.54 g	Saturated fat
17.5 g	Carbohydrate	4 mg	Cholesterol

Diabetic exchanges: Starch, 1; lean protein, 1¼

Lemon Cookies and Cream Dessert

Quick and easy, this will satisfy your sweet tooth.

1 box (0.3 ounces) sugar-free lemon Jell-O
1 cup boiling water
1 tub (12 ounces) fat-free cream cheese
¼ teaspoon vanilla
4 tablespoons Equal sweetener
16 vanilla wafers, slightly crushed

Combine sugar-free lemon Jell-O with boiling water and stir until dissolved. Set aside to cool. In food processor, mix cream cheese, vanilla, and sweetener until smooth. Gradually add Jell-O and process to mix thoroughly.

Lightly crush 8 vanilla wafers and sprinkle over bottom of pie plate or 8-inch round or square dish. Pour lemon mixture over crushed wafers. Crush 8 more wafers and sprinkle over top. Refrigerate about 1 hour and serve chilled.

Recipe makes 8 servings.

Each serving provides:

102	Calories	1.2 g	Fat
13.1 g	Protein	0.28 g	Saturated fat
10.2 g	Carbohydrate	8 mg	Cholesterol

Diabetic exchanges: Starch, ⅔; lean protein, 1

Peaches and Cream Dessert

———❦———

Cool and creamy . . . wonderful peach flavor.

1 can (15 ounces) sliced peaches packed in fruit juice, do
    not drain
$^3/_4$ cup fat-free cream cheese
$^1/_2$ teaspoon vanilla
$^1/_2$ cup skim milk
1 package (1 ounce) fat-free sugar-free white chocolate
    instant pudding mix
Nonfat nonstick cooking spray
$^1/_3$ cup graham cracker crumbs

In food processor, combine peaches with juice, cream
cheese, and vanilla. Process until well blended. Add skim
milk and pudding mix, and process for 1 minute. Spray
8 × 8-inch dish with cooking spray. Sprinkle graham
cracker crumbs on bottom of dish. Gently pour peach
mixture over cracker crumbs. Refrigerate for a few hours
before serving. This is a spoonable dessert. It does not set
up to cut into wedges.

Recipe makes 9 servings.

Each serving provides:

71	Calories	0.4 g	Fat
3.8 g	Protein	0.11 g	Saturated fat
12.5 g	Carbohydrate	4 mg	Cholesterol

Diabetic exchanges: Fruit, $^3/_4$; lean protein, $^1/_2$

Lemon Sour Cream Cake with Cream Cheese Frosting

Doris is a huge fan of lemon *anything*, and this cake is one of her favorites!

Cake
1 cup cake flour
1 1/2 teaspoons baking powder
1/2 cup Equal sweetener
2 tablespoons powdered buttermilk
1/4 teaspoon Sweet 'n Low sweetener
1/4 cup sugar
1/2 stick margarine (1/4 cup), slightly softened
1/4 cup fat-free liquid egg product
1/3 cup lemon juice
1 teaspoon lemon extract
1 teaspoon vanilla
1/2 cup fat-free sour cream
Grated peel from 1 lemon
Nonfat nonstick cooking spray

Cream Cheese Frosting
1 tub (8 ounces) fat-free cream cheese
1/4 cup Equal sweetener
1/2 teaspoon vanilla
1/2 teaspoon Molly McButter dry butter flavor sprinkles*
1 tablespoon lemon juice
1/4 teaspoon lemon extract

*This can be found in small bottles in the baking supplies section of the market.

Preheat oven to 350 degrees F

In large bowl, combine flour, baking powder, Equal sweetener, powdered buttermilk, Sweet 'n Low sweetener, and sugar, and stir until well blended. Add margarine, egg product, lemon juice, lemon extract, vanilla, sour cream, and grated lemon peel, and mix with electric mixer. Spray 9-inch square baking dish with cooking spray. Pour batter into baking dish and bake at 350 degrees F for 35 minutes. Test center of cake with toothpick for doneness. Remove from oven and cool.

In medium bowl, combine all ingredients for frosting and beat with electric mixer until smooth. Spread over cooled cake.

Recipe makes 9 servings.

Each serving provides:

216	Calories	5.2 g	Fat
22.4 g	Protein	1.38 g	Saturated fat
18.6 g	Carbohydrate	5 mg	Cholesterol

Diabetic exchanges: Starch, 1; lean protein, 2½

Orange-Apricot Coffee Cake

Fix this for your resident morning grouch. There's something just so cheery and upbeat about oranges and apricots at breakfast!

Nonfat nonstick cooking spray
2 cups reduced-fat Bisquick baking mix
1 1/4 cups skim milk
2 tablespoons sugar
1/4 cup frozen orange juice concentrate, thawed
1 teaspoon vanilla
1/4 cup fat-free liquid egg product
3/4 cup Smuckers light apricot preserves
2 tablespoons Equal sweetener, for top after baking

Preheat oven to 350 degrees F

Spray bundt pan with cooking spray. In large bowl, combine baking mix, skim milk, sugar, orange juice concentrate, vanilla, and egg product. Mix thoroughly. Pour half of the batter evenly into bundt pan. Spoon a small amount of apricot preserves on top, going all the way around the batter. Try to place the preserves so there will be some in every bite. Pour the remaining batter on top. Bake at 350 degrees F for 40 minutes. After removing from oven, turn out on cooling rack and sprinkle top with Equal sweetener.

Recipe makes 10 servings.

Each serving provides:

176	Calories	1.6 g	Fat
6.1 g	Protein	0.34 g	Saturated fat
34.0 g	Carbohydrate	1 mg	Cholesterol

Diabetic exchanges: Starch, 2; fruit, ¹/₄

Orange Poppy Seed Cake

——❦——

Luscious orange flavor!

Cake
1 cup cake flour
1 1/2 teaspoons baking powder
1/2 cup Equal sweetener
1/4 teaspoon Sweet 'n Low sweetener
1 1/2 tablespoons powdered buttermilk
1/4 cup sugar
1/2 stick margarine (1/4 cup), slightly softened
1/4 cup fat-free liquid egg product
1/3 cup skim milk
1/4 cup frozen orange juice concentrate, thawed
1 teaspoon vanilla
1 teaspoon orange extract
2 teaspoons poppy seeds
2 tablespoons fat-free sour cream
Grated peel from 1 fresh orange
Nonfat nonstick cooking spray

Glaze
1/3 cup frozen orange juice concentrate, thawed
1/2 teaspoon vanilla
3 tablespoons Equal sweetener

Preheat oven to 350 degrees F

In large bowl, combine flour, baking powder, sweeteners, powdered buttermilk, and sugar. Mix with spoon until thoroughly blended. Add margarine, egg product, skim milk, orange juice concentrate, vanilla, orange extract, poppy seeds, sour cream, and grated orange peel, and mix with electric mixer. Spray 8-inch baking dish with cooking spray. Pour batter into baking dish and bake at 350 degrees F for 35 minutes. Test center of cake with toothpick for doneness.

In small bowl, mix ingredients for glaze thoroughly with spoon. Pour over warm cake.

Recipe makes 9 servings.

Each serving provides:

232	Calories	5.6 g	Fat
18.0 g	Protein	1.43 g	Saturated fat
27.4 g	Carbohydrate	1 mg	Cholesterol

Diabetic exchanges: Lean protein, 1½; fruit, 1; starch, 1

Peanut Butter Pie

—✦—

This tastes wonderfully decadent! A few years ago while in Philadelphia, we ate at the Old Original Bookbinders, where we were introduced to peanut butter pie. We decided that if we ever make it to heaven, there will probably be Bookbinder's peanut butter pie for every meal. Until then, here's our own no-guilt version of a heavenly dessert. This pie is best when served the same day it is made. Its appearance deteriorates on the second day.

1 box (1.2 ounces) Jell-O sugar-free vanilla cook-and-serve pudding and pie filling
2 1/2 cups skim milk
1 tub (8 ounces) fat-free cream cheese
1 teaspoon vanilla
2 tablespoons smooth peanut butter
4 tablespoons Equal sweetener
1 baked and cooled pie crust*

Topping
1 tub (8 ounces) fat-free cream cheese
4 tablespoons Equal sweetener
1 teaspoon vanilla

*We like Pillsbury Pet Ritz frozen pie crusts. They are quick and easy to use and have only 4 grams of fat per serving. If you do not want to use a frozen pie crust, use 1/3 cup graham cracker crumbs mixed with 1 tablespoon Equal, sprinkled on bottom of pie plate. This will lower the fat by 2 grams per serving.

In medium bowl, combine pudding mix and milk. Microwave using cooking times on package. Set aside to cool, stirring pudding a few times while cooling.

In another medium bowl, combine cream cheese, vanilla, peanut butter, and sweetener. Use electric mixer and blend until smooth. Add pudding and mix thoroughly. Pour into baked pie shell and chill for 1 to 2 hours.

While pie chills, mix cream cheese, sweetener, and vanilla for topping using electric mixer. When pie is firm, gently spread topping over pie and return to refrigerator to chill about another hour.

Recipe makes 8 servings.

Each serving provides:

244	Calories	6.2 g	Fat
24.7 g	Protein	1.99 g	Saturated fat
18.7 g	Carbohydrate	14 mg	Cholesterol

Diabetic exchanges: Lean protein, 3; starch, 1

Peach Pockets

——✦——

Yummy!!! A fruity little dessert bundle!

Nonfat nonstick butter-flavored cooking spray
1 can (15 ounces) sliced light peaches, well drained and
    cut in half
1 teaspoon Molly McButter dry butter flavor sprinkles*
1/2 teaspoon vanilla
4 tablespoons Equal sweetener
1 tablespoon corn starch
Dash of cinnamon
4 eggroll wrappers**

Preheat oven to 400 degrees F

Spray large baking sheet with cooking spray. In medium
bowl, combine all ingredients except eggroll wrappers.
Stir with spoon to mix. Using a dinner plate for a work
surface, place one wrapper on plate. Place one-fourth of

*This can be found in small bottles in the baking supplies section of the market.
**These are usually found in the produce section of the market.

peach mixture in center of wrapper. Fold the bottom corner up and over peach mixture and continue folding like a small package. Place on baking sheet. Repeat procedure for remaining eggroll wrappers. Spray tops with cooking spray. Bake at 400 degrees F for 14 minutes.

Recipe makes 4 servings.

Each serving provides:

166	Calories	0.0 g	Fat
15.3 g	Protein	0.00 g	Saturated fat
27.0 g	Carbohydrate	0 mg	Cholesterol

Diabetic exchanges: Starch, 1½; lean protein, 1

Pineapple Upside-Down Cake

———— ❧ ————

One of our favorites! Hide this from the rest of your family. We do not turn ours upside down but serve it out of the baking dish. However, you can turn yours upside down if desired.

Bottom Layer
Nonfat nonstick cooking spray
1 can (8¼ ounces) crushed pineapple, do not drain
½ teaspoon Sweet 'n Low sweetener
¼ teaspoon vanilla

Cake
1 cup cake flour
1½ teaspoons baking powder
½ cup Equal sweetener
½ teaspoon Sweet 'n Low sweetener
1 tablespoon powdered buttermilk
½ stick margarine (¼ cup)
¼ cup fat-free liquid egg product
¼ cup sugar
⅓ cup skim milk
1½ teaspoons vanilla

Preheat oven to 350 degrees F

Spray an 8-inch square glass baking dish with cooking spray. In small bowl, combine ingredients for bottom layer and stir with spoon. Pour into baking dish and spread evenly.

In medium bowl, combine cake flour, baking powder, sweeteners, powdered buttermilk, and mix with spoon. In another medium bowl, combine margarine, egg product, sugar, skim milk, and vanilla, and beat with electric mixer. Add flour mixture and blend well with electric mixer. Pour batter over pineapple mixture in baking dish. Bake at 350 degrees F for 35 to 40 minutes. Remove and cool.

Recipe makes 9 servings.

Each serving provides:

176	Calories	5.3 g	Fat
12.9 g	Protein	1.39 g	Saturated fat
19.0 g	Carbohydrate	1 mg	Cholesterol

Diabetic exchanges: Starch, 1; fruit, $1/2$; lean protein, 1

Deluxe Pineapple Cream Pie

———✺———

A lush, creamy pie that's a snap to make. Like all cream pies, this pie is best when served the same day it is made. Its appearance deteriorates after the first day.

Pie
2 1/4 cups skim milk
1 package (1.2 ounces) Jell-O sugar-free vanilla cook-
    and-serve pudding and pie filling
1 tub (8 ounces) fat-free cream cheese
1 teaspoon vanilla
4 tablespoons Equal sweetener
1 can (8 ounces) crushed pineapple, do not drain
1 baked and cooled pie crust*

Topping
1 tub (8 ounces) fat-free cream cheese
1 teaspoon vanilla
4 tablespoons Equal sweetener

In medium bowl, combine milk and pudding mix and cook in microwave or on stove top following cooking instructions on package. Set aside to cool, stirring a few times while cooling.

*We like Pillsbury Pet Ritz frozen pie shells. They are quick and easy and have only 4 grams of fat per serving. If you do not want to use the frozen pie crust, use 1/3 cup graham cracker crumbs mixed with 1 tablespoon Equal, sprinkled on bottom of pie plate. This will lower the fat by 2 grams per serving.

In another medium bowl, combine cream cheese, vanilla, and sweetener. Mix with electric mixer until smooth. Add crushed pineapple with juice and mix. Add pudding and blend. Pour into baked pie shell and chill for 1 to 2 hours.

While pie chills, combine ingredients for topping. Use electric mixer and blend until smooth. After pie has chilled for at least an hour, spread topping on it and return to refrigerator to finish chilling.

Recipe makes 8 servings.

Each serving provides:

233	Calories	4.2 g	Fat
23.5 g	Protein	1.59 g	Saturated fat
21.3 g	Carbohydrate	14 mg	Cholesterol

Diabetic exchanges: Starch, 1¹/₂; lean protein, 2; fruit, ¹/₂

Pineapple Cream Pie

—✦—

We are crazy about this pie! The rich, creamy filling makes us feel that we are really indulging! Like all cream pies, this pie is best when served the same day it is made. Its appearance deteriorates after the first day.

1 box (1.2 ounces) Jell-O sugar-free vanilla cook-and-serve pudding
2¼ cups skim milk
1 tub (8 ounces) fat-free cream cheese
⅓ cup Equal sweetener
1 teaspoon vanilla
1 can (8 ounces) crushed pineapple, do not drain
1 (9-inch) frozen pie crust, baked and cooled*

Cook pudding according to box directions using skim milk. Set aside to cool, stirring occasionally.

*We like Pillsbury Pet Ritz frozen pie shells. They are quick and easy and have only 4 grams of fat per serving. If you do not want to use the frozen pie crust, use ⅓ cup graham cracker crumbs mixed with 1 tablespoon Equal, sprinkled on bottom of pie plate. This will lower the fat by 2 grams per serving.

In medium bowl, combine cream cheese, sweetener, and vanilla. Beat with electric mixer until smooth and creamy. Mix in canned pineapple. Add pudding to cream cheese and pineapple and stir with spoon. Pour into baked and cooled pie crust. Chill for 1 to 2 hours and serve.

Recipe makes 8 servings.

Each serving provides:

190	Calories	4.2 g	Fat
15.5 g	Protein	1.59 g	Saturated fat
20.2 g	Carbohydrate	9 mg	Cholesterol

Diabetic exchanges: Starch, $1^{1}/_{3}$; lean protein, 1; fruit, $^{1}/_{2}$

Creamy Pistachio Dessert

———✎———

Cold and refreshing, this is always a popular dessert!

1 tub (12 ounces) fat-free cream cheese
¼ teaspoon vanilla
6 tablespoons Equal sweetener
2 cups cold skim milk
1 package (1 ounce) sugar-free instant pistachio pudding
22 lowfat chocolate wafers (like vanilla wafers)

In food processor, combine cream cheese, vanilla, and sweetener. Process until smooth. In medium bowl, combine cold milk and pudding mix, and whip or beat for 2 minutes. Pour into food processor with cream cheese mixture and process until thoroughly mixed.

Line bottom of 8-inch round or square dish with 20 chocolate wafers. Save 2 wafers to crumble and garnish top. Pour pudding mixture over wafers. Sprinkle top with wafer crumbs. Chill about 1 hour and serve.

Recipe makes 9 servings.

Each serving provides:

131	Calories	0.7 g	Fat
15.8 g	Protein	0.06 g	Saturated fat
13.6 g	Carbohydrate	8 mg	Cholesterol

Diabetic exchanges: Starch, 1; lean protein, 1

Raspberry Coffee Cake

—— ✦ ——

Unique coffee cake with a delicious raspberry center.

Nonfat nonstick cooking spray
2 cups reduced-fat Bisquick baking mix
1 ¼ cups skim milk
¼ cup sugar
1 teaspoon vanilla
¼ cup fat-free liquid egg product
¾ cup Smuckers red raspberry light preserves
1 tablespoon Equal sweetener

Preheat oven to 350 degrees F

Spray bundt pan with cooking spray. In large bowl, combine baking mix, skim milk, sugar, vanilla, and egg product. Mix thoroughly. Pour half the dough evenly into pan. Distribute small spoonfuls of raspberry preserves on top of dough, evenly around the pan. Try to place preserves so that each bite will have preserves in it. Pour the remaining dough on top. Bake at 350 degrees F for 40 minutes. Remove cake from pan when done and turn out on cooling rack. Sprinkle top with 1 tablespoon Equal sweetener.

Recipe makes 10 servings.

Each serving provides:

156	Calories	1.6 g	Fat
4.6 g	Protein	0.34 g	Saturated fat
30.7 g	Carbohydrate	1 mg	Cholesterol

Diabetic exchange: Starch, 2

Pumpkin Pie Deluxe

———❦———

Great for the holiday season!

1 can (15 ounces) pumpkin
$^1/_2$ cup fat-free liquid egg product
1 $^1/_2$ teaspoons vanilla
1 teaspoon Molly McButter dry butter flavor sprinkles*
$^1/_3$ cup evaporated skim milk
$^1/_4$ cup flour
$^3/_4$ cup Equal sweetener
$^1/_4$ teaspoon Sweet 'n Low sweetener
$^1/_2$ teaspoon Brown Sugar Twin
$^1/_2$ cup fat-free sour cream
1 tablespoon pumpkin pie spice
Dash of ground cloves
1 frozen Pet Ritz pie crust, thawed**
$^1/_4$ cup chopped pecans, optional
2 tablespoons Equal sweetener to sprinkle on top of
    baked pie

*This can be found in small bottles in the baking supplies section of the market.

**These crusts are only 4 grams of fat per serving. We like to take frozen pie crust out of foil pan while it is still frozen and place it in a 9-inch pie plate sprayed with cooking spray. Let stand until thawed, then gently press crust to fit pie plate.

Preheat oven to 350 degrees F

In large bowl, combine pumpkin, egg product, vanilla, butter flavor sprinkles, skim milk, flour, sweeteners, Brown Sugar Twin, sour cream, pumpkin pie spice, and cloves. Mix with electric mixer until well blended. Pour filling into unbaked pie crust and sprinkle pecans evenly over top, if desired. Bake at 350 degrees F for 45 to 50 minutes. Check center of pie with knife for doneness. If it comes out clean, it is done. Let pie cool about 10 to 15 minutes and then sprinkle top with Equal sweetener.

Recipe makes 8 servings.

Each serving provides:

217	Calories	4.3 g	Fat
25.8 g	Protein	1.64 g	Saturated fat
17.8 g	Carbohydrate	3 mg	Cholesterol

Diabetic exchanges: Starch, 1; vegetable, 1; lean protein, 2

Pumpkin Squares with Orange Cream Cheese Icing

What wonderful flavors! Don't limit this to Thanksgiving . . . it's good anytime!

Crust
Nonfat nonstick cooking spray
16 vanilla wafers, crushed

Filling
1 can (15 ounces) pumpkin
$\frac{1}{2}$ cup fat-free liquid egg product
$\frac{1}{4}$ cup Brown Sugar Twin
$\frac{1}{4}$ cup fat-free sour cream
$\frac{1}{2}$ teaspoon Molly McButter dry butter flavor sprinkles*
1 teaspoon vanilla
$2\frac{1}{2}$ teaspoons pumpkin pie spice
2 tablespoons flour

Frosting
1 tub (8 ounces) fat-free cream cheese
$\frac{1}{2}$ teaspoon vanilla
$\frac{1}{4}$ cup frozen orange juice concentrate, thawed
4 tablespoons Equal sweetener

*This can be found in small bottles in the baking supplies section of the market.

Preheat oven to 350 degrees F

Spray 8-inch square glass baking dish with cooking spray. Sprinkle crushed vanilla wafers evenly over bottom of dish. In large bowl, combine all ingredients for filling except flour. Use an electric mixer to thoroughly mix. Gradually add the flour while continuing to mix. Gently pour filling into dish over vanilla wafer crumbs. Bake at 350 degrees F for 40 minutes. Remove and cool.

In medium bowl, combine all ingredients for frosting and mix with electric mixer until smooth. Spread over top of cooled pumpkin cake. Cut into squares.

Recipe makes 9 servings.

Each serving provides:

146	Calories	2.4 g	Fat
12.3 g	Protein	0.65 g	Saturated fat
18.5 g	Carbohydrate	5 mg	Cholesterol

Diabetic exchanges: Starch, 1; lean protein, 1; vegetable, 1

Raspberry Sweet Rollers

—✥—

Great idea for a snack!

Nonfat nonstick butter-flavored cooking spray
4 eggroll wrappers*
4 tablespoons Smuckers red raspberry light preserves
4 tablespoons Equal sweetener
2 teaspoons Molly McButter dry butter flavor sprinkles**

Preheat oven to 400 degrees F

Spray baking sheet with nonstick cooking spray. Using
large dinner plate for work surface for wrappers, place
a wrapper on plate and spread with 1 tablespoon raspberry preserves. Sprinkle 1 tablespoon Equal and
$1/2$ teaspoon butter flavor sprinkles over preserves. Start
at one corner of wrapper and roll up like a pencil. Place
roll on baking sheet and repeat procedure for remaining
wrappers. Spray tops of each roll with cooking spray.
Bake at 400 degrees F for 9 minutes.

Recipe makes 4 rolls. One serving equals 2 rolls.

Each serving provides:

154	Calories	0.0 g	Fat
14.9 g	Protein	0.00 g	Saturated fat
24.0 g	Carbohydrate	0 mg	Cholesterol

Diabetic exchanges: Starch, $1^1/2$; lean protein, $1/2$

---

*These are usually found in the produce section of the market.

**This can be found in small bottles in the baking supplies section of the
market.

Pineapple Cream Cake

———&———

A moist cake with delicate flavors. . . . We love it!

Nonfat nonstick cooking spray
1 box (8½ ounces) Estee pound cake mix*
1 can (8 ounces) crushed pineapple, drained
¾ cup fat-free sour cream
¼ teaspoon almond extract
¼ cup Equal sweetener
½ teaspoon vanilla
1 egg white
½ cup water

Preheat oven to 350 degrees F

Spray 8-inch square glass baking dish with cooking spray.
In large bowl, combine all ingredients and mix with electric mixer. Pour batter into baking dish and bake at 350
degrees F for 35 to 40 minutes. Be sure to test center of
cake before removing from oven. Cool and serve.

Recipe makes 12 servings.

Each serving provides:

119	Calories	1.7 g	Fat
6.2 g	Protein	0.84 g	Saturated fat
19.4 g	Carbohydrate	0 mg	Cholesterol

Diabetic exchanges: Starch, 1; lean protein, ½; fruit, ¼

---

*Estee cake mixes are sweetened with fructose, not artificial sweetener, so
they are fairly high in carbohydrates.

Chocolate Silk Pie

—✧—

This makes a yummy chocolate dessert.

1 tub (8 ounces) fat-free cream cheese
$^1/_2$ cup fat-free sour cream
1 teaspoon vanilla
$^1/_2$ cup Equal sweetener
1 box (3 ounces, two envelopes) Sans Sucre lowfat chocolate mousse mix
1$^1/_4$ cups skim milk
1 (9-inch) Pillsbury Pet Ritz frozen pie crust, baked and cooled*

In medium bowl, combine cream cheese, sour cream, vanilla, and sweetener. Beat with electric mixer until smooth. In large bowl, combine both envelopes of chocolate mousse mix and skim milk. Beat with electric mixer for 5 minutes, starting out on low and working up to

*We like Pillsbury Pet Ritz pie crust for this recipe. If you do not want to use a frozen pie crust, use $^1/_3$ cup graham cracker crumbs mixed with 1 tablespoon Equal, sprinkled on bottom of pie plate. This will lower the fat by 2 grams per serving.

highest speed on mixer. Gently fold cream cheese mixture in with mousse mixture, using a spoon. Stir until well blended. Pour into baked pie crust and chill about 1 hour or longer if desired.

Recipe makes 8 servings.

Each serving provides:

226	Calories	6.6 g	Fat
19.3 g	Protein	2.55 g	Saturated fat
19.0 g	Carbohydrate	9 mg	Cholesterol

Diabetic exchanges: Starch, 1; lean protein, 2; skim milk, $^1/_2$

Tropical Fruit Pie

———— ✢ ————

This is fabulous. . . . Doris loves the tropical fruit flavor.

Fruit Filling
1 envelope Knox unflavored gelatin
$1/4$ cup water, boiling
1 tub (12 ounces) fat-free cream cheese
1 teaspoon vanilla
$1/4$ cup Equal sweetener
1 can ($15^1/4$ ounces) Dole tropical fruit salad in light syrup
    and passion fruit juice, do not drain
1 can (8 ounces) crushed pineapple, do not drain

Crust
$1/3$ cup graham cracker crumbs
1 tablespoon Equal sweetener
Nonfat nonstick cooking spray

Dissolve unflavored gelatin in boiling water. In medium bowl, combine cream cheese, vanilla, and sweetener. Mix with electric mixer until smooth. Using a spoon, fold in tropical fruit salad with juice and crushed pineapple with juice. Stir gently until well blended. Stir in dissolved gelatin.

In small bowl, combine graham cracker crumbs and sweetener, and mix. Spray 9-inch pie plate with cooking spray. Sprinkle graham cracker crumbs evenly over the bottom. Gently pour pie filling over graham cracker crumbs. Chill 2 to 3 hours before serving.

Recipe makes 8 servings.

Each serving provides:

144	Calories	0.4 g	Fat
14.9 g	Protein	0.11 g	Saturated fat
18.0 g	Carbohydrate	8 mg	Cholesterol

Diabetic exchanges: Starch, 1; fruit, 1

Chocolate Mousse Cheesecake

Out of this world!

Crust
Nonfat nonstick cooking spray
¹/₄ cup graham cracker crumbs
2 tablespoons Equal sweetener

Filling
2 tubs (12 ounces each) fat-free cream cheese
³/₄ cup fat-free sour cream
1 envelope (1¹/₂ ounces) Sans Sucre sugar-free lowfat
    chocolate mousse
1 teaspoon vanilla
³/₄ cup Equal sweetener
¹/₂ teaspoon almond extract
¹/₈ teaspoon light salt

Spray 9-inch pie plate with cooking spray. In small bowl, mix ingredients for crust. Sprinkle this mixture over bottom and sides of pie plate. In large bowl, mix cream cheese with electric mixer until smooth. Add sour cream and mix well. Add mousse mix, vanilla, sweetener, almond extract, and salt, and mix with electric mixer until smooth and creamy. Gently spoon mixture into pie plate, trying not to disturb crust. Chill 1 to 2 hours and serve.

Recipe makes 8 servings.

Each serving provides:

213	Calories	1.5 g	Fat
34.8 g	Protein	0.58 g	Saturated fat
10.5 g	Carbohydrate	15 mg	Cholesterol

Diabetic exchanges: Starch, $^1/_2$; lean protein, 3

Chocolate Banana Cream Dessert

Doris created this recipe, but it *belongs* to Alice! This is the most heavenly dessert we have eaten in a long time. Yum!

16 reduced fat chocolate wafers (like vanilla wafers)
1 box (0.9 ounces) Jell-O instant sugar-free banana cream pudding
1 ½ cups skim milk (for banana pudding mix)
1 large banana, sliced
1 tub (8 ounces) fat-free cream cheese
¼ cup Equal sweetener
1 teaspoon vanilla
1 box (1.4 ounces) Jell-O sugar-free chocolate cook-and-serve pudding
2 cups skim milk (for chocolate pudding mix)

Line bottom of 8-inch square glass baking dish with chocolate wafers. Prepare banana cream pudding according to package directions. Fold in sliced banana and pour this mixture over chocolate wafers. In medium bowl, blend cream cheese, sweetener, and vanilla. Beat with electric mixer until smooth and creamy. Pour this mixture over the layer of banana cream pudding. Prepare chocolate pudding following package directions, then cool and stir occasionally for about 15 minutes. Pour this mixture on top as last layer. Chill 1 to 2 hours and serve.

Recipe makes 9 servings.

Each serving provides:

140	Calories	0.7 g	Fat
12.9 g	Protein	0.14 g	Saturated fat
19.9 g	Carbohydrate	6 mg	Cholesterol

Diabetic exchanges: Starch, 1; fruit, $^1/_2$; lean protein, $^1/_2$

Chocolate Cake with Fudge Frosting

Comfort cake. . . . Need I say more?

Cake
1/3 cup cocoa powder
1 cup cake flour
2 teaspoons baking powder
1 tablespoon powdered buttermilk
1/2 cup Equal sweetener
1/4 teaspoon Sweet 'n Low sweetener
1/4 cup sugar
1/4 cup liquid egg product
1/2 stick margarine (1/4 cup), slightly softened
1/3 cup skim milk
2 teaspoons vanilla
1/2 teaspoon Molly McButter dry butter flavor sprinkles*
2 tablespoons fat free sour cream
Nonfat nonstick cooking spray

Frosting
1/4 cup mini chocolate chips
1/2 cup lowfat evaporated skim milk
1 teaspoon vanilla
1/2 teaspoon Molly McButter dry butter flavor sprinkles*
1/4 teaspoon Sweet 'n Low sweetener
1 tablespoon sugar
1/4 cup fine chopped pecans, optional
1/2 cup Equal sweetener

*This can be found in small bottles in the baking supplies section of the market.

Preheat oven to 350 degrees F

In large bowl, combine cocoa powder, cake flour, baking powder, powdered buttermilk, sweeteners, and sugar, and stir with spoon until mixed thoroughly. Add egg product, margarine, skim milk, vanilla, butter flavor sprinkles, and sour cream, and mix with electric mixer until smooth. Spray 8-inch square baking dish with cooking spray. Pour in batter and bake at 350 degrees F for 30 minutes. Test center of cake with toothpick for doneness. Remove and cool.

In medium saucepan, combine all ingredients for frosting, except Equal sweetener. Cook and stir constantly and cook over medium heat. When mixture comes to a boil, continue stirring and cooking for 4 minutes. Remove from heat and add Equal sweetener; stir until cooled a little. Pour frosting over cake after the cake has cooled for 10 to 15 minutes.

Recipe makes 9 servings.

Each serving provides:

262	Calories	7.3 g	Fat
25.7 g	Protein	2.57 g	Saturated fat
24.6 g	Carbohydrate	2 mg	Cholesterol

Diabetic exchanges: Starch, 1$\frac{1}{2}$; lean protein, 2; skim milk, $\frac{1}{3}$

Index

Bran muffins
  almond, 2–3
  apple, 4–5
  date and nut, 17
  pumpkin, 24–25
Breads. *See also* Biscuits; Muffins
  cheese, garlic and poppy seed
    with, 20
  cinnamon crisps, 11
  corn fritters, 16
  cream cheese rolls, orange
    glazed, 14–15
  dilly, 18–19
  garlic cheese toast, 21
Breakfast casserole, 102
Breakfast sausage gravy and
    biscuits, 176–177
Broccoli
  and rice, cheesy, 38–39
  salad, 37
Brownie sour cream cake, 224
Burrito, Tex-Mex, 196–197
Butter. *See* Lemon butter
Buttermilk chicken, 179
Buttery rice bake, 103

C

Cabbage
  and meat pie, German, 96–97
  sweet and sour, 80
Cakes
  almond, sweet, 210–211
  brownie sour cream, 224
  carrot, with cream cheese
    icing, 222–223
  cherry swirl, 238–239
  cherry upside-down, 226–227
  chocolate, with fudge frosting,
    282–283
  cranberry-orange bundt,
    242–243

  lemon sour cream, with cream
    cheese frosting, 250–251
  orange poppy seed, 254–255
  pineapple cream, 273
  pineapple upside-down,
    260–261
Cantaloupe with orange cream
    sauce, 33
Carrot
  cake, 222–223
  orange, 64
  raisin salad, 40
  soup, velvety, 49
Casseroles
  apricot curried chicken,
    116–117
  beef and bean ranch bake,
    90–91
  biscuit bake, hearty ranch,
    150–151
  breakfast, 102
  chicken and dressing, 108–109
  chili corn bake, 114
  family, 186–187
  French toast, overnight, 124
  hominy green chili cheese
    bake, 57
  lasagna, ultra lowfat, 122–123
  macaroni and cheese, 126
  potato, creamy, 48
  potluck, 168–169
  rice bake, buttery, 103
  rice pilaf, 149
  tortilla, 200–201
Cheddar cheese
  breakfast eggs with, 120
  broccoli and rice with, 38–39
  chicken with, crispy, 118
  garlic toast with, 21
  veggie biscuit loaf, 28–29
Cheese
  bake with spinach, 180

sour cream cake with cream
cheese frosting, 250–251
Lemon butter, fresh asparagus
in, 59
Lemon sauce, chicken breasts
with, 182–183
Luncheon chicken salad, 125

M

Macaroni
  cheese and, 126
  salad, curry, 53
  salad, picnic, 62
Meatloaf, old-fashioned, 127
Meats. *See* specific types
Mexican chicken and noodles,
  128–129
Mozzarella cheese
  and American cheese pie,
    104–105
  garlic and poppy seed bread
    with, 20
  hearty skillet breakfast,
    142–143
Muffins. *See also* Breads
  almond bran, 2–3
  apple bran, 4–5
  apricot, 8
  banana, 6–7
  banana nut, Doris's, 9
  chocolate chip orange, 30–31
  date nut bran, 17
  pumpkin bran, 24–25
Mustard
  baked chicken with, 119
  chicken with honey and,
    188–189

N

Noodles
  and chicken, Mexican,
    128–129

spicy, 148

O

Oklahoma okra, 63
Old-fashioned beef stew,
  156–157
Old-fashioned gravy, 22–23
Old-fashioned mashed potatoes,
  60–61
Old-fashioned meatloaf, 127
Onions, green beans with
  roasted, 66–67
Orange
  -almond chicken, 190
  -apricot coffee cake,
    252–253
  beef and vegetable stir fry,
    130–131
  carrots, 64
  -cranberry bundt cake,
    242–243
  cream cheese icing, pumpkin
    squares with, 270–271
  cream sauce, fresh cantaloupe
    with, 33
  glaze, cream cheese rolls with,
    14–15
  muffins, chocolate chip, 30–31
  poppy seed cake, 254–255
  sweet potatoes, crispy, 84
Oriental cucumbers, 65
Oriental peanut salad, 78
Oven French fries, 55
Overnight French toast
  casserole, 124

P

Paprika chicken, 132–133
Pasta. *See also* Noodles
  primavera, 134–135
  tomato and basil, 178

and vegetables, Italian,
136–137
veggie sauce, 81
Peaches
cream dessert, 249
pockets, 258–259
Peanut butter
-chocolate cream pie,
234–235
pie, 256–257
Peanuts
chicken on rice, oriental,
164–165
chicken salad with, spicy,
72–73
oriental salad with, 78
Pea salad, crunchy, 68
Pepper chicken, 199
Pepperoni pizzas
mini, 144
rolls, 138–139
Pepper steak, 140–141
Picnic macaroni salad, 62
Pies
banana cream, 220–221
beef and potato, 92–93
cheese, baked, 104–105
cherry chocolate chip,
228–229
chocolate cream, supreme,
236–237
chocolate-peanut butter
cream, 234–235
chocolate silk, 274–275
coconut cream, 240–241
lemon chess, 246–247
meat and cabbage, German,
96–97
peanut butter, 256–257
pineapple cream, 264–265
pineapple cream deluxe,
262–263
pumpkin deluxe, 268–269
tropical fruit, 276–277

Pineapple
cream cake, 273
cream pie, 264–265
cream pie deluxe, 262–263
upside-down cake, 260–261
Pistachio cream dessert, 266
Pizzas
crust, 145
pepperoni
mini, 144
rolls, 138–139
rolls, 142–143
Pockets
peach, 258–259
sweet cherry, 225
veggie, 76–77
Poppy seeds
garlic and cheese bread, 20
orange cake, 254–255
Pork
smothered, potatoes and, 163
tenders in gravy, 146–147
Potato
and beef pie, 82–83
casserole, creamy, 48
French fried, oven, 55
and ham chowder, cheesy,
42–43
hearty skillet breakfast,
152–153
layered bake, 172–173
mashed, old-fashioned, 60–61
new, and green beans, 56
salad, dilly, 54
salad, southern, 82
skins, restaurant-style, 83
smothered pork and, 163
sweet, crispy orange, 84
Potluck casserole, 168–169
Puddings
blackberries and, 209
corn, 44
Pumpkin
bran muffins, 24–25

Now You Can Keep Diabetes Under Control

It's simple: If you have type 2 diabetes, the only way to ward off serious symptoms is to keep your blood sugar within acceptable levels. So how can you do it? Through proper nutrition, the master key to controlling blood sugar. You need to understand which foods to eat, when to eat them, and in what amounts, and at the same time, establish regular exercise habits to optimize your health.

Inside is everything you need to know about managing type 2 diabetes through proper nutrition. From how to handle the initial diagnosis to discussions on every major dietary component, you'll uncover the science behind treating diabetes the right way.

THREE RIVERS PRESS

Available everywhere books are sold.
Visit us online at www.crownpublishing.com.

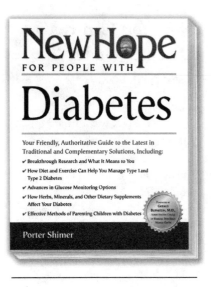